Praise for *Cracki*

"Mergers and acquisitions are John's passion. When I met him in his twenties he was already more knowledgeable about this field than most people. A decade later he is truly an expert in the field and has guided our firm and clients through hundreds of M&A transactions. This book is a must read for anyone looking to execute a transaction in this arena. We can all learn from his experience and passion for the entrepreneurial spirit."

Julie Ayers, CPA, CGMA, CCIFP
Partner at LB&A, Certified Public Accountants, PLLC

"Thank God John Bly was around during my last M&A since *Cracking the Code* was not. *Cracking the Code* is like reliving the process all over again. It amazes me how clear, plain and simple John and this book makes the M&A process."

Dan Wilson
President/CEO of Waypoint IT Experts, EO Charlotte President

"John Bly has worked with dozens of our clients over the years and in every instance has made a major impact on their business. He has represented both buyers and sellers on such important matters as structuring a transaction from a debt and equity perspective, guiding them thru the complexities of the tax laws when one sells their business, to even helping our clients find ways to grow their businesses. John is an astute businessman and his experience in growing his own business through merger and acquisition gives him a unique prospective for advising people on M&A matters. This book should be read by every business owner, prospective business owner and their advisors!"

Brad Offerdahl
President of VR Mergers & Acquisitions, Charlotte, NC

"This book covers an important topic, and there aren't very many good books out there on it. John, a student in my EMP Class of 2015, captures the essence of M&A as it relates to entrepreneurs; in language that is easy to understand, and more importantly easy to execute."

Verne Harnish

CEO of Gazelles, author of Mastering the Rockefeller Habits *and* The Greatest Business Decisions of All Time

"John Bly's expertise as a successful and resourceful entrepreneur shines in this new book. As a long time, trusted referral partner for our clients, John has consistently demonstrated the ability to integrate strategic buy and sell side vision and guidance into all of his engagements. Having personally experienced the rewards and challenges of organic and strategic growth from the perspective of a corporate executive as well as a private sector consultant to small business owners, I find this book to be an essential roadmap for ensuring that your small business stays ahead of the growth curve through the continual evaluation and prudent execution of sound growth strategies via mergers and acquisitions."

Trevor Crocker

Senior Advisor at VR Mergers & Acquisitions

CRACKING the CODE

CRACKING the CODE

An Entrepreneur's Guide to
**GROWING YOUR BUSINESS THROUGH
MERGERS AND ACQUISITIONS**
for Pennies on the Dollar

JOHN BLY
CPA, CVA, CGMA

Advantage®

Published by Advantage, Charleston, South Carolina.
Member of Advantage Media Group.

ADVANTAGE is a registered trademark and the Advantage colophon is a trademark of Advantage Media Group, Inc.

Printed in the United States of America.

ISBN: 978-159932-427-2
LCCN: 2013952003

This publication is designed to provide accurate and authoritative information in regard to the subject matter covered. It is sold with the understanding that the publisher is not engaged in rendering legal, accounting, or other professional services. If legal advice or other expert assistance is required, the services of a competent professional person should be sought.

 Advantage Media Group is proud to be a part of the Tree Neutral® program. Tree Neutral offsets the number of trees consumed in the production and printing of this book by taking proactive steps such as planting trees in direct proportion to the number of trees used to print books. To learn more about Tree Neutral, please visit **www.treeneutral.com**. To learn more about Advantage's commitment to being a responsible steward of the environment, please visit **www.advantagefamily.com/green**

Advantage Media Group is a publisher of business, self-improvement, and professional development books and online learning. We help entrepreneurs, business leaders, and professionals share their Stories, Passion, and Knowledge to help others Learn & Grow. Do you have a manuscript or book idea that you would like us to consider for publishing? Please visit **advantagefamily.com** or call **1.866.775.1696**.

To my wife, Darci, who started this entrepreneurial journey with me in 2004 and has to live with all the crazy things I say and do: thanks for trusting in me and giving me a long leash to run with.

To my girls, Anna, Avery and Ainsley, who might still be too young to know all the crazy things I do: Daddy loves you more than you will ever know, and don't ever let anyone tell you that you can't do something.

ACKNOWLEDGMENTS

I couldn't possibly mention everyone who has had a significant impact on my life and led to my writing this book, but I'm going to give it a shot. To those I have forgotten: I'm sorry, and next time I see you, I'll owe you a drink.

I would be remiss if I didn't provide a special acknowledgment to my parents. No two parents in the world are as incredible as they are. They have been the rocks for me throughout my entire life. They both were employees and I always thought I got my entrepreneurial spirit from my friends at Bryant University. However, in writing this book I had an epiphany: I really got it as a kid from my parents and didn't know it. It was a moment of catharsis. As a kid, I plowed snow, delivered papers for years, and even sold slices of pizza at summer camps. My parents still love to tell the story of the time I went away with Paul Demkowski for a week to camp with about $300 in spending money and came back with $500.

My appreciation also goes to other folks who have had an enormous impact on my life: my partners at LB&A, Julie Ayers, Courtney LaLone, Chris Chesson, Dave Frasier, Jim Lovell and the entire team at LB&A, for allowing me to continue to come up with crazy ideas and, as a team, for building with me an incredible firm with amazing people; the Entrepreneurs' Organization (EO)—

all the members and leaders who have had an impact on me over the years—for being one of the best things that ever happened to me; my forum at EO Everest, both past and present members, for being an incredible knowledge-sharing crowd, with each member impacting my life in so many positive ways that I can't even recount them; Adam Witty, the publisher of this book and an EO forum-mate of mine, for inspiring me many times about the opportunities books provide and for being the first person who made me think it was possible; Greg Crabtree, for his leadership in the book-writing process and for showing me the way; Cameron Herald, for the painted picture idea; Tom Weddell, an incredible managing partner of a remarkable CPA firm in New York, for being a mentor of mine; my management of an accounting practice group without whom I surely would have failed years ago; Bryant University, for providing me the best education money can buy and for the many friends there who created so many lasting memories, including watching all of my closest friends' families take journeys through entrepreneurism, especially Steve Manocchio, Mike Cucinnota, Mike Ehrich and the rest of the PIT crew; Vistage and my group, for all the support and knowledge sharing; Entrepreneurial Masters Program (EMP) taught at MIT outside of Boston, and my class of 2015, for all the leadership and guidance; EO Leadership Academy Class of 2012, for the leadership in both personal and business training and sharing; Jay Offerdahl, for all the friendship and joint M&A work over the years; Dana Bradley, for providing me with a leadership path in EO and for paving the way for EO Charlotte.

ABOUT THE AUTHOR

John Bly, CPA, CVA, CGMA is the founding partner of LB&A, and his entrepreneurial leadership has propelled its growth. LB&A ranks sixteenth in the *Charlotte Business Journal's* Top 25 CPA Firms in the Charlotte Region. John and his wife created Bly & Bly, CPA, with the purchase of Carolina Professional Accounting in 2004. Since then, there have been a total of ten mergers and acquisitions that have transformed the firm into its present state.

John steers the firm's consistent growth of personnel and expansion of client services. In 2004 the firm offered bookkeeping and tax services. Now the firm has expanded to include services such as assurance services, government audit, business valuations, merger and acquisition consultation, peer review, controller services, tax planning, wealth management, accounting for charter schools and a variety of entrepreneurial growth services. With six partners and over thirty professionals, John continues to grow the firm both organically and through acquisitions. His strategic plan led to a second office in Greensboro to serve the rapidly growing Greensboro/Triad market.

John spends his time regularly consulting on 20–30 merger and acquisition (M&A) transactions a year, both on the buy side and the sell side. He is seen as an expert among his peers and has spoken to CPA firms in Raleigh; Pinehurst, Nebraska; and West Virginia to help them grow an M&A practice. Additionally, he regularly works with business brokers and investment bankers to help structure and plan deals, not just from a tax perspective but from the perspective of culture and planning for strategic growth.

John's professional influence reaches far into the business community. His role in business development continually expands LB&A's service radius. John is a frequently requested presenter who is called upon to share business ideas and growth strategies. His emphasis on proactive strategic growth has earned him a reputation as a thought leader in the business community in all matters of taxation and mergers and acquisitions, and he has created a network of professionals to enable emerging entrepreneurs. John has a passion for listening, learning and transferring knowledge through consultations with corporate clients. His leadership locally and globally in Entrepreneurs' Organization has earned client and peer accolades.

Of the many awards and recognitions earned by John, the most notable include a national award for the M&A Advisor 40 Under 40 for 2013, the 2013 Accounting Today Award Recipient for Managing Partner Elite, the *Charlotte Business Journal's* Forty Under 40 for 2011, and the *Charlotte Business Journal's* Top 25 CPA Firms in the Charlotte Region for the years 2007–2013.

John not only believes in the growth of the firm but the growth of himself professionally. He has continued this process over the last few years by acquiring multiple additional licenses, which include Certified Public Accountant, Certified Valuation Analyst, Chartered Global Management Accountant, Series 7 General Securities Representative, and Series 66 Uniform Combined State Law.

He is also part of several different organizations and groups around Charlotte including the Entrepreneurs' Organization (EO),

Vistage, Firm Foundation Advisory Board, Association for Corporate Growth (Charlotte Chapter), American Institute of Certified Public Accountants, and National Association of Certified Valuation Analysts.

In EO, John is seen as a leader and has served on the local board of this global organization of more than 9,000 members for four years. In addition to his EO presidency in 2011, he has served on the Global Standing Finance and Audit Committees as well as the Eastern Regional Council, and was chairman of the largest regional conference in EO history. Currently, John is attending the MIT Entrepreneurial Masters Program (class of 2015) and he is an EO Accelerator speaker and facilitator, helping high-growth companies.

To learn more about John and working with LB&A, Certified Public Accountants, please visit www.cparesults.net.

FOREWORD

This book is a must read for those who are living the American Dream and those who are pursuing it. When people ask me why I believe so highly in John Bly, I tell them John is an entrepreneur who happens to have an accounting degree. It is rare to have a trusted advisor who has been in your shoes, walked the walk and put his financials where his mouth is.

In business transactions, we often find buyers and sellers taking advice from their respective counselors (accountants and attorneys mainly) who have zero knowledge of real-world experience for which they receive fees. When John advises on buy side or sell side, he speaks from the perspective of someone who has walked in that client's shoes. This real-world experience is what he shares in his book *Cracking the Code*.

If every buyer and seller read this book prior to engaging my services, my job would become much easier.

Jay Offerdahl

VR Mergers & Acquisitions, member EO Charlotte

TABLE OF CONTENTS

WAY TO GROW!

I was 25 years old when I embarked on an odyssey of growth. The CPA firm that I founded struck deals for two small acquisitions in 2004, another in 2005, and two large ones the following year. In a two-year period, we did $1.7 million worth of deals and bought $600,000 worth of real estate with close to no money down.

I tell you this not to demonstrate that I'm all that amazing, but rather, to let you know that you could do it too. You don't need to have half a million or a million dollars down to grow your business through mergers and acquisitions.

What's most important is to have the desire—and a strategy and structure to make it happen. If you have that, you can take your company to new heights with explosive growth, and you can do it with a minimum amount down, and perhaps not even a dollar out-of-pocket. We recently finished one such deal.

Every business should have an exit strategy. You might sell the company. You could close it and walk away, or transition it within the family. You need a strategy, and it should be in your mind when you start your company and for every decision going forward. Without a strategy, you might not end up where you want to go.

You have to have some idea of your game plan, whether for 5 or 15 years or longer. You don't have to have all the details, but you should know your trajectory. When you can envision your growth and exit strategy, you will be able to base all your decisions on it, including acquisitions.

Doing What You Do Best

Most entrepreneurs started their business because they wanted to be their own boss. It allowed them to express their creative side. Often they find that they can greatly enhance that creativity and dramatically build the business through mergers and acquisitions.

It's a way to grow while you focus on what you are good at, instead of having to deal directly with accounting, budgeting, sales, or human resources. If you can get big enough to support employees in those positions, you can reach a point where you're doing just the things you want to do. And that's when growth really takes off.

In this book, we'll take a close look at how that process works. By acquiring other firms with complementary skills, services or products, a business can quickly grow and allow its owners to focus on what they enjoy about the business, and it can give them more time to enjoy life, as well.

Through mergers and acquisitions, an entrepreneur can rapidly grow from one or two employees into a good-size, middle-market business. The growth sometimes is 20 percent, 50 percent, even 100 percent. It's fairly easy to then build support structures in a way that you couldn't do at a growth of 5 or 10 percent a year. With that support in place, you can focus on the reason you got into the business in the first place.

The Fast Lane to Success

Considering how many small businesses fail, you wouldn't start one unless your tolerance for risk was reasonably high. Just the sound of "mergers and acquisitions" can seem intimidating, as well, but consider this: Businesses that grow to a revenue of $1 million, the statistics show, rarely fail. Only about 4 percent of businesses in the United States reach that point, but it's a critical mass that, once reached, tends to secure success.

Mergers are a faster way to reach that critical mass. If you have a one- or two-person business, your next hire represents a 30 to 50 percent growth. That first hire can feel like a struggle, since, as the owner, you sometimes can't take that step backward in pay, but after several hires the percentage by which each new hire increases the staff becomes much smaller and more manageable, and the next hire isn't nearly as hard. M&A becomes a highly efficient way of growing by leveraging what you have already.

It might seem complicated, but if you break down the process of mergers and acquisitions into its elements, it's quite doable. You just need to take it one bite at a time. If you think you could never acquire a two-million-dollar company, then you're never going to acquire one. If you think you can, you can. Either way, you're right.

You can follow clearly defined steps to accomplish the goal, and a positive attitude is what it takes to move forward on those steps. You need to consider numerous elements, such as whether the company cultures are a good match. Is everybody going to play nice in the sandbox? Do the financials work? You are responsible for the due diligence that will help to ensure wise decisions along the way.

If you take it piece by piece, you can eliminate potential M&A prospects and get down to the ones that are a good fit for you. In the right deal, one plus one might equal three or four or five. In a bad deal, one plus one could equal 1.5.

Huge Rewards

Let's get started, because the rewards are huge. Smart businesspeople know when they need to get help, and help is available to navigate the M&A process. Steering that ship can be relatively simple, but a good captain needs a worthy crew who know the ways of the sea.

Growth through M&A can be simple and lucrative, if you focus, first, on whether the firms are a good fit. First come the fundamentals. Is this company a good match for you? Do the numbers work? Are you sure this is a practical and not an emotional decision? You may identify some issues that you will need to work through but that shouldn't stop the deal. If you can handle the risk, it's a big opportunity to grow. If you can't get past the risk, you're not going to get to the closing table on a deal.

Our company is a great example of M&A by strategy. We've grown from zero to over four million in nine years through eight acquisitions and two mergers. Other firms that have started from scratch cannot grow that fast without doing acquisitions. No matter what the industry, it's next to impossible to grow by 50 to 100 percent year over year.

A lot of people think that the numbers are the biggest part of an M&A transaction. But as I will soon explain, I don't think that's the most important part. I think the corporate cultural fit is more important. Just because the numbers seem to make sense doesn't mean the organizations will complement each other. In the business news, we regularly see examples of deals that went awry because of cultural incompatibility.

Nonetheless, by following some basic rules, you can do this over and over and realize amazing growth. Success stories abound. Clearly, mergers and acquisitions are part of the game in the business world.

Entrepreneur's Growth Guide

By acquiring smaller companies, you can quickly get to the size where you could sell for multiples of what the individual acquisitions cost. Let's say you can buy three or four companies for $3 million, perhaps three times earnings. But once you've combined them and your total worth is over, say, $10 million, you then might be able to sell them for five times earnings. You may not have improved the business model. You may have just found four complementary businesses and instantly had a significant return on your investment.

There are lots of books out there on private equity groups and big mergers and acquisitions. This book is for the entrepreneurial business owner with $1 million to $30 million in revenue. Let me show you ways to find potential spots for rapid growth and accomplish, on a smaller scale, what the bigger companies are doing.

It can take a business a lot of time and effort to add individual customers, but when you buy a significant number of them all at once through M&A, you gain significantly even if you lose a few of them. If you have done your due diligence, you will be acquiring a customer base that was loyal to its owner and will be loyal to you, as well. That way, you have profits from the start.

It's not uncommon to hear the buyer worry that those new customers will vanish because they liked the old owner so much. The reality is that most customers don't like change, and they don't care who owns the company. To them, finding another vendor is much more complicated than transitioning to the new buyer. They end up staying, in large percentages, because it's easier.

Help for Buyers, Sellers and Advisors

This book is for both buyers and sellers. It is for entrepreneurs considering the acquisition, merger, or the sale of a company. It is for those who want to grow a company significantly by using M&A as a strategy or want to make the most of it in a sale. I believe that the same due diligence that leads to a good purchase also leads to a good exit. Again, you have to have the end in mind. If the end that you have in mind is to always have a lifestyle business and never have an exit, then this book isn't for you.

Bankers and attorneys will find information of value in this book, as well, to help entrepreneurs with such deals. This book will help advisors to see the whole picture beyond the numbers. One plus one might equal five if the cultural mesh is favorable, but a banker who is just dealing with the financials might not see that. This book will encourage advisors to ask questions about culture, new markets, and opportunities that could open up. And it will encourage advisors to look beyond the risk their client faces. Instead of killing deals, they should be able to see when a deal could be transformational for their client.

This book is not written for the expert. It is written as an easy read for those who are taking those steps for the first time. It could be their first acquisition, or maybe the second or third, and maybe they have made mistakes along the way and want to get better at it and learn a repeatable process and system.

Entrepreneurial businesspeople are typically founders or cofounders or at the start of the second generation. Perhaps they just bought a first business. Such businesses tend to be in the $1 million to $30 million range. In the United States, it's hard to break through those numbers without rapid growth or a lot of acquisitions.

Businesses with that kind of revenue are highly underserved in the M&A world. The owners don't look at M&A as a strategy. They're not looking for five, separate, million-dollar deals. They're not soliciting or getting advice. They don't always have a CPA or attorney who is familiar with doing such deals. This book is designed for entrepreneurs in that range.

My goal is to keep it simple. I am presenting information in layman's terms, not in the lingo of investment bankers who spout terms that ordinary readers likely won't understand.

A Roadmap to Prosperity

The typical clients we've worked with vary greatly. We've worked with staffing agencies, distribution companies, and heavy inventory businesses. We've looked at software-as-a-service providers, a rapidly growing market over the last four or five years. They are getting significant returns on exits.

We've also helped IT companies, both managed-service providers and product providers. We've worked in the health-care industry. We've worked with two or three health-care companies that continue to acquire both products and patents.

We have worked also with construction companies. Those deals can be more difficult, since such companies often are seen as working from project to project without a recurring client base. However, companies that have a significant niche or expertise can be a good acquisition for a buyer who wants to grow in that specialty.

This book can help businesses trying to design an exit strategy. If you have a business that is not today in an industry or in a position that would command the type of money you'd like out of an exit, this book will give you the steps to put it in that position in the next three, five, or seven years. You will learn in these pages what a buyer is likely to be looking for, and what you must do to attract that interest.

Your growth will certainly be among those attractions. I want to reach those people who are looking to get to the next level. That next level may be growing from half a million to a million, or from four million to ten million. The next level may be expanding into new skill sets. The strategies outlined in this book can help you grow to a sustainable size. You can be one of the few that reach the range of $1 million to $30 million in revenue, at which point statistics show you are likely to thrive.

In short, I am reaching out to those who have found some solid success and are ready to build upon it but don't quite know how. The steps have been done over and over again by successful businesses. I am confident that I can help show you the way, simply, clearly, and without the jargon that confuses so many. If you are one of those business men or women, you will find a roadmap here for growth as you build for a prosperous future.

Who We Are

I am the founder and managing partner of LB&A, Certified Public Accountants, PLLC. We have a different niche in the world, in that we're good at mergers and acquisitions in our own business, which allows us to be even better advisors. We also have a unique branding item. We work with clients almost exclusively on fixed pricing, and not on hourly rates. That's made a big difference for us in our markets.

I think of myself as an entrepreneur who is dumb enough to be a CPA. I'm part of the Entrepreneurs' Organization, which has more than 9,000 members worldwide. I've spent a lot of time around entrepreneurs. When I describe myself as an accountant, that doesn't sound entrepreneurial, but I have found that you can make any profession entrepreneurial.

We are a CPA firm with a perspective that I believe is unique. We're not just advisors. We did 10 M&As ourselves between 2004 and 2013, and we considered and analyzed well over 80 other deals for ourselves in that period. As I write this, we are working on three other potential deals.

We look at growth in a way that is rare among small to midmarket companies. They're looking at who their next customer is or what the next market may be. We redefine entrepreneurialism in a way that amplifies growth and strengthens our trajectory.

I think about where we were nine years ago with two people who did everything and compare that with today, when our employees and partners can spend much more time on the things they do best. We have seen the kind of growth that keeps people happier.

We now have offices in Matthews, near Charlotte, NC, and in Greensboro, NC. Our vision in the near term is to stretch the corridor from Richmond, VA, to Columbia, SC so that we become a regional firm. We're a full-service CPA firm, providing wealth management, business valuations, M&A consulting, CFO and controller-type work, outsourced accounting, audited financial statements and tax consulting, tax planning, and tax returns.

We advise on 20 to 30 merger-and-acquisition deals a year, some for buyers and some for sellers. Our clients might be buyers who have engaged us to help with due diligence, or are in the early stages and haven't found a company yet but want to understand what to look for. In cases like that, we might do a consulting project and consider the firm's needs and what might be a good fit. Other clients might be selling a company and sometimes our advice might be to not sell—not yet. "Maybe you should do an acquisition yourself and get a little bit bigger," we might say, "and then look at an exit in three to five years when you have sustainability."

Most of my own time with our firm is focused on M&A with our larger projects and engagements. I have the passion and the skills for those deals and have done many of them in the past decade. We have others who help out on the projects, but all of the transactional work at the high level goes through me as well as the consulting related to it.

We recently finished a deal in which the client's accountant couldn't move quickly enough. The client reached out to us through an investment banker with whom we've done a lot of deals and knew we understood the process and could make the deal happen faster. We helped with some accounting records and the due diligence.

Waypoint is a managed-service IT company that had been using a smaller CPA firm that didn't have any merger experience. The owner got to spend a lot of time with me through the Entrepreneur's Organization. We spent a few days together at a conference in Hong Kong, and afterward, he contacted me for help with a transaction that took him from just under $1 million to almost $2 million overnight. It transformed his business. It allowed him to do more business development and high-level client service and get out of being a technician. We worked through significant debt and restructure issues, ownership issues, culture fit and systems issues. We did that over a period of six to nine months. That was a few years ago and the business is now thriving.

Several years ago we worked with a roofing company on a potential sale. The buyer didn't have the right type of counsel. It was a transaction worth about $3 million. The way the original deal was structured would have cost the roofing company nearly $1 million in tax. We were able to eliminate about $600,000 of that tax through the transactional structure. The buyer got to write off the value over a longer period of time, which meant our client got capital gains instead of ordinary income, which made a significant difference. Tax considerations are central to a good deal, and we'll be taking a closer look at that in Chapter 5.

An Interest Became a Passion

My interest in mergers and acquisitions grew as I became involved in our own transactions in 2004 and 2005, and I found that interest becoming a passion. I loved the culture fit. I loved the due diligence. I loved the negotiations and working out the details of the deals. I realized that this could be good not only for our personal growth but for our clients too. Having experienced the process ourselves, we could say, "Listen, We've done it ourselves. As your advisor, we're standing on the front line with you."

In 2008 I got involved in the Entrepreneurs' Organization. To be a part of that group, you have to be the founder, cofounder, or majority decision maker of a business doing more than $1 million of revenue. The nonprofit was started 26 years ago to help people learn and grow. It's not about doing business with other members, but rather, it's about sharing experiences, what you've been through that might help others grow their businesses or avoid pitfalls.

In my years with EO I've found that the more you give, the more you get. I currently stand on the global finance committee, which gives me oversight of the entire organization and its direction and vision. I've been fortunate enough, over the last year, to be what they call an accelerator facilitator, working with high-growth businesses to reach that million-dollar threshold that only 4 percent of businesses attain. Thirteen percent of the Accelerator Program's graduates reach that level, however.

I have an undergraduate degree from Bryant University, of which Jack Welsh wrote, "I've known as many great leaders from Bryant University as I have from the Ivy League schools." Bryant is a private university focused purely on business in the Northeast. I then got a full scholarship to the University of Denver to do my graduate work in taxation.

I'm currently enrolled in the Entrepreneurial Master's Program, a joint venture between the Entrepreneur's Organization and MIT outside Boston. That's a three-year program for rapid-growth companies, helping them put structures, systems and processes in place to solidify that growth. I regularly attend learning events with people who have an insatiable growth appetite. I have a passion for working with people who are trying to grow their businesses, and for helping those who are struggling.

I enjoy people, and particularly people with big ideas. I enjoy interacting with them and helping them to negotiate a meeting of minds. After meeting someone, I often hear the comment: "You don't seem like a CPA!" When they see that I deal with a lot more than numbers, they get engaged in the conversation. I do indeed feel like the entrepreneur who was dumb enough to be a CPA.

I serve in alliances with CPA-firm managing partners through-out the country. I have discussed our success in M&A and have had the opportunity to consult with several firms across the country on doing such deals themselves and helping their clients do them.

In the Pages Ahead

This book will begin with a look at company culture and fit. I consider that to be the most important topic. We'll look at management style, accountability, integration, people issues, operational issues, locations and offices and business systems. For M&A to succeed, these matters must be addressed first. As you will soon see, this book is about a lot more than taxes and the cost of the deal. If you can't get past the fit, it doesn't matter how good the numbers are.

Then we'll take a look at the details of due diligence, examining the concerns that must be addressed up front. As you get deeper into due diligence, you might learn that what had seemed to be a good match has some troubling aspects to it. We did a deal in 2006 where everything on the surface seemed great. The work was good. The people were good. The pricing was fine. We acquired this firm but later realized the owner had put it on autopilot for six months and left us with a big backlog of work. It was still a good deal, but you wouldn't think you'd have to look behind desks and in drawers and dig through things to find the mess. Since then, we have looked even deeper during due diligence.

We'll look at structuring the deal to make it beneficial to both parties. There's no such thing, in the M&A world as a win-lose situation, unless the seller has to sell for some significant personal reason. That doesn't happen often. We'll look at details of the financing, and whether the deal is doable by both parties. We'll talk about stock deals, and earn-outs, and transitions and more. We'll be looking at the many considerations in structuring the deal.

As for valuation, what methods do businesses use? You often hear about EBITDA (earnings before interest, taxes, depreciation and amortization). In reality, EBITDA is extremely helpful for companies that are large, with audited financials that private equity groups are buying. But sales of businesses valued in the $1 million to $10 million range are typically based on cash flow, which is not necessarily indicative of net income. There are things that can be looked at in a different way to produce cash flow.

We'll see how tax considerations can have a lot to do with how a deal is structured. We can save clients a significant amount of money. It's the party with experience on its side that will find itself doing better with taxes. We have significant expertise. Clients often want to know how much they'll get to keep when the deal is done, and that depends a lot on the business structure and the effectiveness of counsel.

In the pages ahead, we'll also be looking closely at the deal flow itself: How do you find the deals, whether through a broker or on your own. Where do you look for prospects? Are you using your website? Are you sending them direct mail? Are you finding them at networking events? Are they being referred to you? There are many opportunities to actively pursue prospects, rather than taking a passive approach. We look for the opportunity that nobody else has seen. Maybe you'll be reaching out to a company that doesn't even know it wants to sell. It all can be part of the deal flow.

I offer this book as an all-inclusive guide for the business owner and for the adviser who doesn't always look at the full picture in a merger and acquisition. You will learn the M&A steps, and how to find a prospect. You will see, once you break it down into its elements, that this is hardly a scary topic. It's actually an exciting one, because you will learn how to put your business on a faster track to success. If you truly want to grow, this book is for you.

CHAPTER 1

ARE YOU A GOOD FIT?

Years ago, here in Charlotte, a large bank acquired an investment advisory firm. It was a great firm that had done a lot of good things. It was not necessarily looking for an exit, but the time seemed right. The bank had discussed how the cultures would fit, the potential dollars the sellers could get, and how the clients would be served.

Within five years, the investment firm had pulled back out of the bank. Why? Because neither of them had a long-term vision and strategy for their fit. Were the cultures compatible? Would the employees be happy working together? Would the clients like the new scenario?

The investment firm had been accustomed to being a boutique firm, working in the best interest of the client. The bank, however, wanted to cross-sell lots of things to the investment firm and push products. But in the acquisition, the firm had given up the authority to say no to those types of actions. It had to peddle the bank's proprietary products, which hadn't been the firm's style. It felt as if it had sold its soul.

Every business, at its core, is about its people. That's where it has to start: Is the M&A going to be a good fit? If not, then it's a waste of time to go any further. If you do the deal, you'll just find out later that it was a mistake because your people aren't happy.

Let's take a look, then, at the operational issues that are at the heart of a business and determine how well it will mesh with another. Operation issues involve how we do things: human resources, accountability, culture, vision, and so on. How do things operate within the business? Do people work from home? Do they have to go to an office?

These are day-to-day considerations, not the 10-year financial budget projection. Do those things align with a candidate for merger or acquisition? Would they add value to your company? Why or why not? Are these major concerns or minor ones? Are they things you can live with, or do they represent a roadblock that you can't get past?

Elements of Integration

When you're integrating companies, several key factors can consume a significant amount of time in ensuring that the merger or acquisition goes smoothly. In an M&A, particularly involving entrepreneurs, people often just think about getting the deal to the closing table. And yes, that's an important step.

But before you get to the closing table, you'd better have a well thought-out plan for how you're going to operationally integrate two cultures, two sets of people, two accounting systems, and two IT systems—everything you use to run your firm.

If all of your due diligence and time focuses on getting to the closing table, you might get there and then find yourself wondering, "What am I going to do tomorrow when I wake up?" That can be a scary thought, particularly if it's the first time you thought about how you're going to interact.

You would think such concerns would have been addressed much earlier. Unfortunately, they often are not. People get wrapped up too much in financial due diligence: "Okay, I can afford it, and here's how I'm going to pay the debt back." They don't look at the integration of systems.

You must assess the cultures of the companies. Is your style laid-back? Do you have an open-book management style? Do you have a suit-and-tie style? Do you keep everything behind closed doors? Are decisions all made by one person or on every level? How much authority do individuals have in day-to-day decisions? How much accountability does everybody have? Do you set goals yearly with all of your people? Some businesses are performance based, meaning that good performers are paid better than nonperformers. Is that the way your culture is? Does everyone get the standard of living increase every year?

If you're the seller and all of your people are over 50, and the buyer's people are all under 30, it's going to be a different culture fit. Will your group be answering to people under 30? Are they going to be peers? How is each going to feel about that?

It's not good enough to just hope it will all work out. Hope is not a strategy. Each company has its own living, breathing culture, and understanding those differences is important in a merger or acquisition. You have to work that out up front. You need a plan of action. Otherwise, you might find out later that it's not a good fit, possibly after wasting a lot of time, money and effort. If you don't have a plan for dealing with people's feelings, pretty soon you won't have people.

The integration of cultures can involve something as elemental as where the headquarters will be. Each of the parties may have its own location, or perhaps all of the employees of one party work out of their homes while the other party's employees go to an office every day. Will those who worked from home now have to report to the office? How will they feel about commuting and working by the clock?

If there are multiple locations, one of them has to be the headquarters. How do the people in the nonheadquarters position feel? Do they feel comfortable? Do you include them? Is there good integration between the two offices? Are there hurt feelings among those who were used to being at the headquarters and now are not? How do you make it feel like one firm?

In considering headquarters and locations, you must factor in the cost of moving during your due diligence. In 2006 we did two acquisitions. We went from working out of our homes to working in an office environment. That involved moving equipment, desktop computers, laptops, and furniture. It also involved upgrading infrastructure inside that office space. We almost doubled the number of office staff.

That can be a significant expense. You need to have a budget for moving expenses so that you know whether it's going to cost you $20,000 or $100,000 or whatever is typical in your industry. You could think you negotiated a great deal and then find yourself laying out $50,000 in the first three months and wondering what happened. If you don't have a plan for that, you can be in for quite a surprise.

Which Business Systems Will Prevail?

In looking at each company's business systems and deciding which will be used after the merger, don't take the attitude of "the buyer's way or the highway." That's old school, and it's not the best approach. You need to understand each system, maybe even try both for a time. Spend some time in the seller's office before the merger.

You have to pick the best of each. Entrepreneurs can be prideful people with egos. After all, many started their own company because they thought they could do things better than the boss. It's good to be proud, but don't let that ego get in the way of your business sense: Some systems simply are better than others, and you might find a better one in the company you are joining.

In one of our acquisitions, we adopted the billing system of the other firm. We immediately changed because we recognized that it was better. Even though we are three times the size we were then, we still use some of those billing procedures. It's a good system that we haven't seen in any firm we have acquired since. If we had said, "Oh, they don't know what they're talking about; we're the buyer here," we would have missed that opportunity.

Two systems can't be run simultaneously for long. If you decide to run two systems for a month, two months, four months, that's okay. But not for five years. You will be paying for two software licenses, with different people learning different things. That's hardly efficient.

We recently acquired a firm and knew up front that its tax software was not going to integrate with ours. We decided before we got to the closing table that we would hire a temporary person for four months to enter the firm's data into our system. That way, when we went live, it would all be there. But if we hadn't contacted the software vendors to learn what would transfer, we would have been caught by surprise. Having a good plan, good questions, and taking action saved us and our clients a lot of headaches.

Do you know how you work? Are the processes defined? Maybe not. Maybe everyone just gets the work done. This could be a good time to understand your processes. Go through a checklist. How many processes are there? How do you do things? Is there consistency, or does everyone have a different way? In our firm we have the LB&A way. Everyone manages a process the same way. Otherwise, it would be hard to pick up the work of somebody who had left the company. It's much easier to have one common way in which everybody does things: invoices, serving clients, and even naming of documents.

Defining Who Does What

Some business owners like to control everything. They do tasks that are beneath their skill set, getting involved in administrative, accounting, and HR functions. In assessing another company's style, look at whether that type of control comes from the top or whether the organization is more relationship driven. Are those functions delegated, whether to an outsourced bookkeeper, a controller, or an HR staff? Is there an administrator or office manager who perhaps does a first pass with resumes and interviews? Who makes the hiring decisions? Is that done formally? Small offices can lack oversight when everyone is so busy that duties get done by whoever happens to have the time.

Styles can clash if you're not careful. You must consider those differences when you're putting companies together and trying to assemble ways of doing things. The owner of one company might be something of a control freak who won't let anybody else see the books, does all the hiring and makes all the decisions. The other company might be managed by delegation at appropriate levels. Those cultures don't mesh well and it's hard to put the pieces together. Employees who have experienced a sense of freedom could resent the feeling that they now are being micromanaged. They may no longer have access to data to make decisions. It can amount to culture shock.

A CPA firm that I know well recently merged with another firm. It was a merger of equals. Nobody was truly the acquirer. As they came together, they decided on a managing partner. The managing partner of one firm ruled on every last penny spent at the firm and made all the decisions. The other firm let office managers decide, up to a certain dollar figure, and let the staff decide on software upgrades and other matters. That all changed. To this day, even the partners consult that particular, dominant managing partner before making decisions, even small ones. They hadn't realized the extent to which operations were micromanaged.

Technology

The compatibility of technology—phone systems, computers, software—is another major consideration in deciding whether two companies can merge smoothly. Technology plays a crucial role in today's world but only when things work. Some technologies just don't play well with other technologies.

That is why it's important to look at the technology that each firm is using and check whether it is transferrable. What software do the firms use? Do they use a certain accounting package? Do they use a certain customer relationship management software, a CRM? And if so, how easy is it going to be to get to one system? Whose system is better? Whose is more robust? How will you get historical information from each firm into a new, combined database? Is it easy? Can you do that through an export, say, to Excel or to some sort of database that then can be reimported, or is somebody going to have to spend weeks rekeying this data?

Our firm is paperless. It has been for quite some time. But we've had firms that have not been paperless that have merged into us over the years and we have had to spend weeks scanning all their old paper files into our paperless environment. To plan for that, we can't just say, "Okay, we need an extra one or two administrative people for six weeks." We also need to make sure that the technology is right. Do we have enough servers and server space? How much space are we going to put on the server by adding 300 client files? Do we have to get a new server just to hold them? When you combine companies, you're not just combining human capital; you're combining investments in technology, the platforms and servers, and determining whether they mesh.

An M&A transaction might be the point when it makes sense to buy a new server, integrate printing networks, and so on. Have you been storing data locally, with servers in-house, or do you use a cloud-based environment where those servers are stored in, say, Atlanta or Wisconsin or someplace, but you all have easy access to data from any location via the Internet?

Consider the phone systems too. Will you be able to easily transfer phone numbers? We've had significant issues over the years with phone providers. One telecom company is the main provider in the Charlotte area, but it doesn't operate in all areas. So at times, we've had to lose phone numbers or deal with portability issues on phone numbers as we've combined companies. If you don't plan for that, you might be surprised that people who are used to calling a certain number are no longer reaching you.

All these considerations might feel intimidating, but when you break them down they can be dealt with relatively simply. You can consult with experts, if need be, as any good business person often does. It's all part of the nature of mergers and acquisitions. You are taking the first and biggest step just by posing the question, "Okay, what are you using?" Then you talk to your internal IT person or your IT service provider or your phone service provider or your Internet provider and get answers.

These might not seem like planning issues of major concern, but they can become so if left unattended. When you have merged and you have six or eight people who can't do anything in technology for several days, you're in trouble. Planning prevents that.

Integration of Finances

You must examine how the finances of the merging companies will be integrated. The range of considerations here is broad. It has to do with recordkeeping. It has to do with timekeeping. Do your people have to keep their time, or are they on salary, coming and leaving when they want? It has to do with payroll. It has to do with bank issues. Are you going to use the buyer's bank or the seller's bank? Which is more convenient? Which has more resources? Who has been more helpful through the merger process?

In a merger, what happens to the bank debt? If you have debt from a previous deal or a line of credit, you should talk to your bank ahead of time and make sure that changing the ownership structure of your company doesn't put you in default. Does the debt need to somehow be retitled? What must be done when you transfer the debt into the combined entity and give up some ownership interest?

Again, people often don't think about such matters. They think, "Oh, it's fine. It's the same company," but the bank looks at it a different way: "Wait a minute, you changed ownership by 20 or 30 percent, so you are in default on this loan because it was agreed that you would notify us ahead of time about any change greater than 10 percent." It's not that they're going to call the loan because you probably are still a good client, but they want to know about it ahead of time. They want to know who they're in bed with. They don't know whether you're randomly putting together a group of bad investors.

You also need to integrate the actual accounting packages, whether you use a large accounting package or something smaller or specific to an industry. You need to come to an understanding about how you keep your finances, whether it's with an owner, a book-keeper or a controller.

When do you do the billing? Is it monthly, quarterly, at the beginning of the month, or as the work is completed? When do clients pay? Do they pay ahead of time or when the bill is given to them? What about receivables and payables? Are you collecting receivables regularly or are most of your clients six months delin-quent? Are you keeping up with your payables or are your vendors unhappy because you're five months behind?

It comes down to deciding which company has best practices and adopting them in the combined organization. If the finances don't work, trouble lies ahead. Cultural issues overall might not fit as well as you would like, but it's important that both parties think about finances the same way.

Intellectual Property

Related to this is intellectual property, such as brand and trade name. What will the company be called after the merger? Those are central issues that need to be decided.

In an acquisition, one company is buying all or most of the value of the other. In a merger, they swap equity for equity, each giving up some of the control. In a true acquisition, the buyer likely won't be changing names, although there are exceptions when the seller has a bigger name or better brand reputation. In a merger, the name can become an issue—and sometimes a big one. Entrepreneurs often don't want to give up the name they created. It represents their legacy. And so, as companies merge, there often is much discussion about what the new name will be. That involves issues of branding and marketing, and whose name is better.

It's hard to measure the return on investment, but you have to get a feel for which company has the better brand or trade name, and which one has the underlying patents. You can't just be stubborn and refuse to give up your name. That kind of ego isn't likely to serve you well. I know a CPA firm that got right down to the end of a deal that almost fell apart on the name issue. They managed to work it out, but it still surprises me that the name can become such an issue even when the parties have agreed on all the rest. This is not a small detail that can wait for the end of the discussions. It's a matter of pride, and pride can play a big role in M&As.

Why Grow?

Growth cannot be just for the sake of growth. When two companies join forces, their cultures should combine in a way that takes both to greater heights for sound business reasons. Two great businesses that had been competitors can then work together to build an even better business. What one company lacked, the other can supply. By combining their skills and products and services, they better serve their clientele.

The corporate cultures have to work together from day one. The smaller the company, the more important the role that culture plays. When companies of fewer than a hundred employees are merging, the fit has to work for every person, every day.

The merger is like dating. At first, you see great possibilities. Then you have some doubts, so you start discussing deeper issues. Most of them are about culture, about who will do what and how you will hold each other accountable. You have to make sure you can live together and act in concert.

Just as a couple comes together and each partner learns about the other and they grow together, so can a business partnership. You're getting to know each other. You're getting to learn each other's habits and ways of doing things and deciding if you can get along for a lifetime. You're marrying your futures and making sure you have what it takes for the long haul.

CHAPTER 2

SO MUCH TO CONSIDER

I recently was working with a staffing company that was considering acquiring another staffing company. The prospect was highly profitable and rapidly growing in a different niche and would have nicely complemented the business. The deal was going through a reputable local investment bank.

The company sent me the financials and information on the business it wanted to acquire. I looked it over and asked myself, "Why are these people selling?" It was a business that had been doubling in size and was profitable, with the owners taking home at least half a million dollars each. "There's got to be something here," I wondered. "What are we missing?"

Before analyzing the cash flow or anything else, I took a 10,000-foot view: What was going on in the industry? It turned out that the

Obama health-care plan could have crippled the business. It was a staffing agency that didn't offer benefits to any of its more than 500 employees. The problem was a gray area for sure—the Obamacare rules still were being written—but the fact the agency wasn't offering benefits provided insight into the sale. With that many employees, a penalty of $2,500 for each employee would amount to well over $1 million.

We didn't know if that was the reason, but the question remained for a potential purchaser: "What if I buy this business and a year later, after the Obamacare rules are finalized, I have to provide coverage? Then I won't be taking home anything because I'll be paying it all to the U.S. government in penalties."

Sometimes in the due diligence process, you can eliminate a target quickly by just asking the right questions. Why are they selling? Maybe there's some hidden reason. There's no point in looking at financials and other details when you've asked some basic questions at a high level and have seen that the deal just won't work.

Within just a couple of hours of easy discussion, we realized the deal wasn't worth doing because of that gray area. There was no reason for further due diligence. "We're not going to get into it," our potential buyer simply said, "because we think there's some concern around Obamacare." As it turned out, the sellers admitted they might have a problem. They thought they could pass off the cost to their customers, but they did acknowledge the risk.

As a CPA firm, we obviously focus on financials, but we go significantly further. We think about the deal from the perspective of both buyer and seller. We've already discussed the elements of a good fit, but what else is involved in ensuring that the clients are satisfied? What does this cost in money and time? What other factors are weighing into the deal? For example, does the seller want out for health reasons?

That all plays into due diligence. In the first round, you might have a standard template of concerns and questions. But as you follow up, you'll take a tour behind the scenes and find out what the business is all about: how it decides things; how it makes its money. Asking the right questions requires an investment of your time, but when the deal gets to the closing table, you will know you have done everything you can to avoid surprises.

Again, it's like dating, but now you're actually looking at the logistics of life together. You're asking questions such as: "Do we combine checking accounts? Do we share how much each other makes? I make $100,000. You make $60,000. Does that mean I should pay proportionately more of the rent? Should I pay more of the bills? Who pays for dinner?"

As a couple contemplates marriage, they sometimes draft pre-marital agreements on how they will be allocating their resources and conducting their financial affairs. Such discussions can forestall a lot of misunderstandings and grief down the road. Will your spouse want to spend all the money or save as much as possible? As you move forward together, the habits of the past should make way for your new priorities together.

You can look at those financial decisions as similar to the due diligence in an M&A. The companies should learn everything they can about each other to assess how they will work out together. In a true acquisition, the buyer won't care if the seller spent money foolishly because that won't continue now. As the new owner, you will have your own agenda. The previous owner's discretionary expenses, foolish or not, will disappear. In a merger, though, both parties will continue and it will be more important to resolve these differences.

Due Diligence Checklist

If due diligence is handled improperly, there's much to lose. LB&A has created a due diligence checklist, which you will find as an appendix to this book for easy reference. In this chapter I will discuss each item on that checklist and its implications. The checklist results from our years of experience in acquiring companies and working with our clients. Most times this can serve as an initial round of questions and items to review, which will lead to more specific direct follow up.

Many times, CPAs look at due diligence as: "I'll take three years of tax returns and financials and see if they make sense." That's just a sanity check. If you can't get past that, you do not want to buy the business. But if you are to make sound decisions as the new owner, you will need a lot more information.

Let's take a close look now at that checklist, which we use with clients to examine the wide range of issues involved.

Nondisclosure Agreement

The checklist starts with what amounts to a nondisclosure agreement. In negotiations, each party will be revealing a lot, and this agreement protects both buyer and seller. The seller wants to know if the buyer will be a good fit for its clients and will be asking plenty of questions to get to the heart of the buyer's way of doing business. If the acquisition fails to go through, that information potentially could be used by the competition. The nondisclosure agreement helps protect against that.

This agreement is a one- or two-page legal document that basically says, "Whatever we share while dating will not be used against each other later." You can find templates for such agreements on the Internet, or you might have your attorney draw one up. It's not all that expensive, but it's important: without that agreement, neither the buyer nor the seller will be likely to want to share much data, and the deal rarely will get far.

The buyer does need to share information with the seller, not necessarily all the financial details, but what will be done with the business and how clients and employees will be treated. The seller's worst fear is that the buyer will shed the clients, fire the employees, and damage the seller's reputation in the community. I've seen that happen, and it makes the buyer and seller look as if they didn't know what they were doing.

Three Years of Tax Returns

The first financial piece we want is three years of tax returns. That seems basic, but the tax returns substantiate the fundamentals. I've seen deals in which a party says he earns $300,000 a year but the tax returns show only $100,000 of net income.

We once had a client who was considering buying a dry cleaner. One of the sellers said, "Well, some of it won't show on the tax returns because those are cash transactions." I told my client, "Well, he kept his cash and didn't report it to the government, so he doesn't get to claim it now." We quickly walked away from that deal.

As they say, you can't have your cake and eat it too. This happens in small business sometimes. It's unfortunate, but it's true. You can't skim money off the top, not report it on your tax return and then think somebody's going to pay three times what you can't prove. It just doesn't happen. So tax returns are a good starting point for buyers to see if what they've been told is close to reality.

Three Years of Financial Statements

Financial statements, many times, can provide much better detail than the tax return. Three years of financials can show you more details of how money actually went in and out of the business. When I say "financials," I mean income statements, balance sheets and, if available, cash flow statements. For smaller businesses, these might be QuickBooks-generated financials. Bigger companies usually have financials that have been audited or reviewed by CPAs.

Even if you have the audited or reviewed financials, you still need to get the internal financials as well for a little more detail. It may indicate what is being done personally through the business. Owners often include expenses that are discretionary. It could be their golf and travel expenses. Maybe they go to five conferences a year. Those are certainly valid business deductions, but you might only go to one industry trade conference.

What you're looking for in the financials are the details of that type of transaction. "I already have a company car," you might say, "so I wouldn't need his company car, obviously." That would eliminate the gas expense of $5,000 or payments of $400 a month. You can start to get a feel for the cash flow you could realize. The current owner might be generating $100,000, but you might see that as $120,000 if, for example, you don't need two office managers. In those three years of financial statements, you are looking for such potential "add-backs," as we call them.

Do the financials reflect what is on the tax returns? If you can fairly easily tie them together, then the company probably does a good job with its books and records. It probably has some good controls in place and a good bookkeeper. If the figures don't tie out, the company may not be working with a good CPA firm, or its internal person isn't paying attention to keeping the books. You can deduce a lot about the internal workings of the company's financial department.

Revenue by Month for Three Years

Then we get into some more financially driven things. What types of revenue peaks and valleys does the company have? I suggest always getting three years' worth of data, but I suggest getting revenue by month and profit and loss by month for a 36-month period. You then may see that the company has busy periods and slow periods.

Is that good? Is that bad? Is it a seasonal business? For instance, in the retail industry, many times companies make money in only the fourth quarter of the year. How does that affect your planning? Does that mean you have to staff up for the fourth quarter? Does that mean you need to have an extra large line of credit to be able to survive those first three quarters?

Perhaps you currently don't have enough business during the fourth quarter, so the merger would result in a perfect sharing and shifting of employees. If their slow season is your busy season, each of you will now be able to better use people's skills. Maybe you don't need twice as many employees. You may find that you have all the staff you need and now your staff have something to do during what used to be the company's slow period.

Salaries per Person

What do you suppose would happen if you took over a business in which the average employee earned $60,000 a year, while you continued to pay your own people $40,000 for the same skill set and performance? You can be sure that people will talk. Maybe not on day one, but within a year or two they will be comparing notes. How do you think employees at the lower pay level are going to feel? That's going to be an awkward conversation.

Pay discrepancy did become an issue in one of our acquisitions, except that it was the seller's employees who were making significantly less. We told those employees upfront they were underpaid. By doing so, we eliminated the behind-the-scenes talk. We told them that they were underpaid according to our model and that we would measure their performance. "We don't know how you perform yet," we said, "but we know how our people perform, and we will make appropriate adjustments quickly. Give us several months to see how you perform." Some of those people did well and got those compensation adjustments. Some performed not as well and didn't get the raise, but they understood why. For comparison, we were able to show them the performance results for those who made more money.

As long as you have those upfront conversations, you can make sense of the pay issue. Otherwise, you will face surprises. You will want to know the details, for example, about hourly pay and overtime and weekend work duties. If you ask questions upfront, you will have better judgment in dealing with salary concerns. You can hurt morale if you do not handle that well.

Staff Duties

Let's say you're taking on a staff of 5 or 10 people. What is each one's role? Is it clearly defined? Is somebody an office manager, and if so, how is that defined? Who does HR? Who handles payroll? Accounting?

Better yet, it's good to get resumes for these folks. We love to see resumes from the company that we are acquiring. You might see an abundance of talent and ask how the company manages to attract such people for the price because, after all, you might want to adopt those hiring practices yourself. Perhaps the perks are what draw these people, or perhaps the job descriptions are particularly attractive.

Look for overlap. Are there two office managers? Could one of them leave or do something else? Maybe one has a finance degree and could become the internal bookkeeper. Maybe one would be better at serving clients, or would be a wiz at marketing. That's why the resumes can be important, because you don't know the employees' backgrounds when you take over. You may find a person with a skill set that would be better applied in a position other than the one he or she has held for 5 or 20 years.

Average Raises

What have the average raises been for the last few years? If your staff is used to 2 percent raises and the new staff is used to 6 percent raises, somebody's going to be surprised next year, one way or the other. If your own employees suddenly find themselves getting a 6 percent raise, they might not be as pleased as you would think. They may be thinking: "Man, have I been getting screwed all these years? Maybe I was in the wrong place. What if I'd have made a change years ago? Is there some other place out there that's giving 6 percent raises?" You have to think about those things. You need to have those discussions.

Recently we helped to negotiate a merger in which the seller hadn't given raises for four years. The buyer had been giving 4 percent raises and made it clear upfront that the new employees would henceforth be getting raises. "That's not a philosophy that we believe in," the buyer told them. Again, you need to be clear from the start on defining salaries and raises. It's not good for the culture if, for example, employees are expecting 6 percent raises and find themselves cut to 2 percent, particularly if nothing is explained.

Bonus Structure

Do the buyer and seller differ on performance-based compensation? Do such bonuses depend on specific goal-setting, accountability, or targets throughout the year? Is that bonus clearly defined? Does hitting those targets trigger, say, a 5 percent bonus? Or is it 10 percent? Or is it nebulous and based on soft skills, in which case, how do you reassure employees that they have control over whether effort equals bonus?

Perhaps the bonus is based on profit sharing. If the company makes more profit, everybody takes more home. There might be a profit-sharing pool that is distributed based on performance. It's important to understand the bonus structure.

Years ago we took over a firm that had a variety of compensation models for employees. During the due diligence phase we asked, "What does the expense reimbursement look like to you? How does that feel?" Their comment was, "It's basically salary, except it's an expense reimbursement."

That was enlightening to us. We didn't see it the same way, but we quickly understood that was how the employees thought of it, so we made a change. We immediately just increased their salaries and got rid of the expense reimbursement. It just made sense. It was the right thing to do.

One particular individual was used to a 25 percent bonus but a lower salary and we asked, "How much of this is performance-based? How much of this is incentive-based or is it really profit-sharing?" That employee replied, "It's nebulous. To be honest, I'm not sure how it's determined but it's been about the same number for the last five years."

To us, that just indicated salary. It didn't sound like any sort of bonus, not in the way that you think of performance-based or profit-based or targets or goals. We elected at that time to put it in the salary because that strategy fit our structure. We said, "That's not the way we do things. To be clear, we'll just put it in your salary, but we want to let you know that there is an incentive comp and here's how you get it. It's not about just showing up. You have to hit these targets. These things have to be done. Some of them are stretch goals. Some of them might be easy to attain."

Again, it's a matter of clarity. You don't know what you don't know, and if you don't ask the right questions at the start, you're going to get lots of wrong answers later.

Benefits

Do the buyer and seller offer the same benefits? What retirement plans are offered? Does one have a 401(k) and the other a Simple IRA? How about health, disability or life insurance? What is the coverage for those sorts of benefits? They're important to people these days.

Many studies have shown that these soft compensations are as important, if not more so, than the actual pay, especially with the rising costs of insurance and other benefits and the rising cost of retirement. Employees expect a 401(k) or some other sort of retirement planning, and the buyer and seller need to be aligned on that.

For example, we took over a company that had a simple IRA and announced upfront that we would continue that for the next year but in year two we would go to our 401(k) model, which allowed greater contributions and more investment options.

We didn't want to make that change right away. Some changes cannot wait, but others can be more gradual, and often people are more comfortable with slower change. They just want reassurance that the buyer will look out for them. In a merger, employees of both companies often are more scared than you might imagine. They worry about the implications for their employment. Good communication upfront helps to smooth the way.

Hourly Billing Rate per Person

Now, let's look at some of the specifics regarding people. For example, with service-based industries, one of the things you'd want to know is how much staff bill out per hour.

If you are acquiring a consulting firm or a law firm or a web design firm or any sort of consulting or professional service industry, generally they bill hourly rates or they track hours and try to get a rate per hour for each individual. You want to make sure those are in line with yours. For instance, if you're paying somebody $50,000 and their billing rate is $70 an hour, how is that going to line up with somebody whose billing rate is $50 an hour? How are you going to make sure that the same work is getting done with the same pricing?

Maybe they're taking longer to get work done. Maybe they're not as efficient. You've got to be aware of those things ahead of time so that you can plan for them. Otherwise, you could be surprised when the hours and rates charged to clients don't line up.

HR Policies

You need to find out about HR policies. Who hires new people? Who does the interviewing? Is there an employee manual or handbook? What does it say? These questions are important as you go through due diligence because you want to make sure that the cultures of human resources line up. If the buyer's doing one thing and the seller's doing another, it can be confusing as you integrate the cultures.

Paid Time Off

Paid time off for vacation, holidays, sick days or personal leave is a key consideration. Is it offered, and to whom—to hourly or salaried people? Is the vacation allotment calculated on a graduated scale, with perhaps 10 days the first year, and 20 days after the third year? Does the employee get, say, three weeks upon the day of hiring, or just one day after three months and another three days at month six?

Is there a certain amount of sick days and vacation days? How are holidays handled? Are the hourly people paid for vacation and holidays or are they just given that time off unpaid?

It's important to find out how these things are done. After you merge, it's hard to run two different compensation models, two different benefit structures, two different time reporting systems. It's much easier to just go with best practices and agree that one of you will change, explaining the reasons to the staff: "Over the next 12 months we're going to go to this model. You'll see why. It's going to be easier. It's going to be better. We can't have people under two different models."

Paid time off can play a major role in your due diligence. If you are buying a company that doesn't offer any vacation and you're used to offering three weeks, what happens when you extend that policy to the new employees? If you are acquiring 10 employees, that's 30 weeks a year that they haven't normally been paid for taking off. That's a significant amount of additional compensation. You may need to hire an extra person to get the work done while these people take vacation. It's important to plan for that.

Owner Perks

You will need to carefully consider the owner perks in the company you are acquiring. You may see a cash flow of, say, $100,000, but how will that change and how many expenses will go away the minute the current owner goes away?

A company car is one example. Perhaps the owner is leasing a company vehicle for his or her own use and you don't need that company vehicle because you may already have one, or you already have a personal vehicle. The minute the current owner goes away, that's going to go away.

The same could be true for other types of expenses, such as country club memberships or dues for certain restaurant clubs, such as the city-club-type of restaurants where they provide fine dining experiences for members. Those go away the minute the owner goes away, which means your cash flow might not be $100,000 a year; it might be $110,000 or $120,000 or $130,000.

Those things are important to determine as you're going through the due diligence process. You want to make sure you can account for them. You need to understand: Is it $5,000, $10,000, $30,000? Is the owner's spouse on the payroll? Is the owner running a big retirement plan for himself or herself through the company? Is the company paying all the owner's health insurance?

What about travel? Is the owner going to exotic conferences for the educational benefits or for the benefits of the locations? Will you continue that?

What about disability insurance? Is the owner running life and disability insurance through the company for personal use? The minute those things aren't needed by the seller, they're going to go away.

We worked through due diligence for a company that ended up not selling a couple of years ago. It was doing about $1 million in profit a year, but when we went through the cash flow items that were add-backs, it ended up being close to $400,000 of add-backs.

These were things such as charitable contributions. That year the company had donated almost $150,000 to the school of one of the owner's children, for example. If you're the buyer of that business, you're clearly not going to donate another $150,000.

On top of that, the owner had purchased multiple vehicles for his own use. They were truly company vehicles, but no single individual needs two or three company vehicles. The owner wanted one in each company location, and there were multiple locations. The owner also had personal whole-life policies in excess of $3,000 a month.

Little things such as meals and entertainment and travel and disability and health quickly can become sizable when you add them up, so remember that owner-discretionary expenses won't necessarily be your own expenses.

Other Insurances

Another consideration is other types of insurance, and not necessarily employee benefits. What is being done with workers compensation liability? What about general liability, professional liability, any sorts of liability that the buyer or the seller may have? You want to understand the risks that you might continue to carry. Is the business doing something that might be fraught with liability? If so, do you have enough coverage?

Underscoring the differences between the buyer's and seller's coverage is important. You may think you know the seller's business model, but once you start looking at the insurance policy you may see that the policy costs twice what yours does and you realize that additional risk involved.

Software

What types of software is the company using? Is it using a customer relationship management, a CRM? Is it using an accounting package? What type of accounting package? Is it a real high-end solution or is it something simple such as QuickBooks or Peachtree? Can it be integrated? There may be specialty software, a special billing and time software related to the managed-service IT industry, for example, or litigation-related software if you're buying a law firm.

Consider whether industry-specific software integrates with your current package. If not, which will you use? How are you going to make sure that all the data transfers easily? In the last chapter I pointed out what could go wrong if you don't attend to that.

It's important to understand software and the costs involved. If you think you will keep yours but learn that you need the other company's software, you could face an expensive upgrade. Getting a handle on that ahead of time is always better than being surprised at the last minute.

Services Performed

What types of services does the other company perform? Is it in the same industry with the same product mix? Maybe you're both in landscaping but one does hardscaping and the other just mows lawns. Are the other company's clients commercial, industrial, or homeowners? All those things are important because you may be entering a product niche or an industry that you have not thought about. You may have a product or a service that you could offer these new clients, whereas the seller didn't have that opportunity.

For instance, we had a landscaping client who was going to sell to a much larger conglomerate that wanted a heavy presence in the apartment and condo industry. The buyer did some hardscape work but needed the large, recurring revenue stream of apartment complexes. Our client was focused in that niche and could provide real value and recurring revenue. You can do well by acquiring a company that complements your own services to expand you client base.

Time Reports for Three Years

Also important, especially for service companies, are time reports. I typically ask for these over a three-year period too. You may not need monthly reports but you do want to see them on a yearly basis. You might learn, for example, that in the company's culture, full-time is only 1,800 hours a year. If you have a growth culture in which your people work 2,300 hours a year, how will you fit together? How will your 2,300-hour people feel when they see the new folks leaving at four o'clock on Thursday and heading out to happy hour at two on Friday? It's just a matter of different cultures, but you might not understand that unless you look at the other company's work hours. That can easily be done, especially in service industries, by looking at time reports for the preceding two to three years.

Receivables

Other financial data to think about, besides just the early financial data we talked about with the tax returns and financials, are the receivables. Specifically, under receivables, you'd like to look at the aging of those receivables, meaning how long the receivables have been out and not collected.

I like to look at three or four time frames over the preceding three years because maybe the other company is busier during certain times of the year than others. Could that mean the company's receivables are higher at certain times? You might need a larger line of credit, but you won't know unless you've seen the numbers, planned for them and made some decisions based on them.

For instance, if the other company's receivables, on average, collect in 20 to 40 days, that's not too bad. But what if there are some Fortune 500-type companies that pay in 60 to 90 days? That'll change your planning for the merger. You might need a larger line because it's going to be 60 to 90 days before you get paid on these big accounts.

Collection Policies

Interrelated to that are the collection policies. How does the other company collect? Does it take credit cards? You might lose 2–3 percent on a credit card, but you could get your money upfront, rather than wait on payment terms of 30, 60 or 90 days. Is the company's policy one of cash on delivery, or does it extend credit terms? If so, does it do any sort of background check, or do all clients get credit until they fail?

That can be expensive. I learned that in 2007. Almost overnight we had gone from being a company doing about $250,000 to one doing about $1.5 million in revenue. That first year we had too much faith in our clients and especially in our new clients, whom we didn't know that well. We got stuck with about $75,000 worth of bad debt. It was a painful lesson as we were rapidly expanding. We realized quickly that we needed to rein in on credit policies, tighten up credit card acceptance, and do more cash on delivery and faster follow-up. It was a lesson I'll never forget, and I hope my readers learn from it.

Billing Policies

When does the other company bill? How often? Does it bill on the first of the month? Does it bill halfway through the month? If it's a big project—say it's a six-month project—does it bill every month? Is billing based on completion times? Maybe there are milestones in a contract whereby a certain percentage of the work has to be done before an invoice can be issued.

The buyer and the seller must come to terms over who has the better practices, who collects money faster, who's able to turn receivables into cash in the bank more quickly and who has a better policy on billing and credit. You need to be open to whether the other party has the fresh ideas you need to improve the business.

List of Equipment and When Purchased

You will want a list of equipment and when it was purchased. You might be in heavy manufacturing, landscaping or IT. Understanding what the capital investment might be as a new owner is important.

For instance, if an IT company leases out servers to clients, what if those servers are three years old? Industry standards might say that servers only last four years. At the end of that first year as the buyer, after you've acquired the business, you may have to invest $30,000, $50,000, $80,000, $100,000 in new equipment.

That could hurt if you didn't understand that upfront. In 2009 I had a client who purchased a company and included in the purchase of the company was the building. My client asked about the physical condition of the building and got all the details. He asked when the roof had been replaced last. He had the impression that it had been replaced seven years previously, with a 15-year warranty. However, he didn't get this information in writing.

Within 18 months the roof had a bad leak. When my client went back to the seller, the seller said, "Oh no, I think you're mistaken. It was replaced 15 years ago with a 7-year warranty." It was quite a problem as my client spent $25,000 repairing a roof he didn't expect to have to replace for eight more years.

You can see that the capital investment that you might have to spend is important to know up front. Don't be surprised, especially in those crucial first 12 to 24 months. You need to understand the financial impact. You're already dealing with a culture change and people change and integration of business. The need for a giant investment on top of that can be daunting.

References

A few other things to check—what I call "softer things"—include reference checks. You might want to check with the Better Business Bureau or other sources to reassure yourself that the party is reputable and that its clients don't just use it because they have little choice. If you have a pristine reputation in the community but the seller doesn't, you could tarnish your own name through the purchase. You could check for lawsuits or references from bankers or vendors. You don't want your reputation to be sullied by association.

Startup Cash Needed

What's the startup cash needed? For instance, if you buy a service-based business and you're buying all the assets of the company, you might have some time before you actually bill and collect on some of the work. You might need three to six months of working capital upfront. Do you have that? If not, do you have a line of credit that could support it?

If you don't have a plan, you could be caught with no cash after 30 or 60 days. Just because the seller's business cash flowed doesn't mean it will from day one under your ownership. You need to understand the cash needed up front. That doesn't mean finding out whether the business will be profitable. You wouldn't be buying it and you wouldn't have gotten to this point if you didn't know it would be profitable. But profit does not equal cash. Sometimes the cash takes a little bit longer to get in.

Inventory

If it's an inventory business, how often is it turning the inventory— three times a year, four, five? It's important to understand how much investment you will have in the inventory that you're carrying and how long it is going to sit.

Research

You should also consider doing some ratio analysis and industry data, particularly if you're unfamiliar with the industry of the company you're acquiring. Perhaps it's an add-on for you.

Risk Management Association provides data for easy research to get industry-conglomerated data based on the size of a company. You can use that data to compare it against the seller's data that you have. That can be helpful just to understand whether it's a growing or dying business and how it is doing against competitors nationwide.

Bank Debt

A final consideration is this: What does the company's bank debt look like? If it's a stock deal, you may or may not be absorbing its bank debt. However, stock deals are rare among the $1 million to $30 million entrepreneurial businesses that are the focus of this book. We'll take a closer look at the details of designing the deal in the next chapter.

Be Prepared—or Surprised

Due diligence could take 30 days. It could take six months. It depends on the size of the business, how much time you have, and how intensely you want to dig into the process. But the longer it takes, the greater the likelihood of what I call "deal fatigue" as both buyer and seller begin to feel worn out. Often the buyer wants to continue but the seller has already checked out and looking to get done with this deal. The seller is not trying to sell the company for the joy of going through a continual selling process. The seller wants to sell and be out.

It is during due diligence when most deals fall apart. They typically fall apart because the buyer has an unrealistic expectation of what the seller's business is. The buyer expects to see a business that's pristine, with no warts, and no issues. That's just not realistic. Every business has its issues. They might be small; only the big ones should get in the way.

This due diligence checklist is meant to be a guide. It doesn't mean that every single one of these items has to be in perfect condition. It just means that you have to prepare for whichever ones are not and make sure that you're making decisions for the combined company in the correct way.

These are the elements that can make the deal go smoothly, or not so smoothly. If you are prepared, you will see those warts for what they are. You will deal with issues and put them in proper perspective. If you're not prepared, expect surprises.

CHAPTER 3

DESIGNING THE DEAL

Many times business owners believe that they have to have $1 million in cash to buy a $1 million business. However, in the summer of 2006, at the age of 27, I was able to close a business for just under $1 million with only 10 percent down and a 10-year note for the remaining 90 percent, at an attractive rate of interest.

If you're reading this, thinking, "Well, John, it's not 2006 anymore. Bank financing like that doesn't exist," I challenge you to get more creative. Since 2009, and the Great Recession, we've seen that banks have tightened. However, sellers still want to get out of their businesses so they're willing to look at options.

Several deals we closed recently have all been owner financed. These terms are still good. They might not be 10-year notes, but they might be 5-year notes or 7-year notes with no money down or 10 percent down. They're payable over a period of time, and instead of owing the bank, you owe another individual.

There are ways to get these deals done. You've gotten past the due diligence. You're ready to do the deal. Now let's dig into how to make it happen. In this chapter, we'll look at designing the deal. This is where the rubber hits the road as you head for the closing table.

As we look at designing the deal, we see there are a few different ways deals get done. They could be cash deals. You could be giving up some equity, in the way of stock. That's most likely the case in a true merger rather than an acquisition. You could have an earn-out. You could have bank debt. You could have owner financing.

We'll discuss all those methods in this chapter, and which one might be best for you. Usually, in a deal there are one or two ways that could make sense and the goal is for buyer and seller to agree on which of those two is best.

It has to be a win-win situation. If it's not, it's likely you're not going to get to the closing table. If you're thinking like a competitive poker player and you're ready to slit the throat of the person on the other side of the table, no deal is likely to happen.

Cash and Stock Deals

In the $1 million to $30 million range, cash deals are uncommon for a number of reasons, not the least of which is that it can be hard to come up with the $500,000 to $5 million in cash needed to close the deal. I've seen it happen, but not often. Only a small percentage of deals are closed that way.

In this value range, stock deals are also few and far between. We'll take a closer look at the reason for that in the chapter on tax considerations. Stock deals usually involve bigger, public companies.

In smaller companies, people often do not want to do stock deals. Yes, that is partly for tax-related reasons, but in this chapter we'll look at other reasons for avoiding such a deal: liabilities. When you're buying the company's stock, anything the previous owner did to upset somebody could come back to haunt you in a liability lawsuit. Does the other party have bank debt? Did it default on a loan or a credit card? All of those things come back to the company and the company's federal ID number and stock.

If you're buying company stock, those things end up becoming your responsibility. Yes, attorneys can draft indemnification clauses, but they are only as good as the paper they are written on and the person who sold you the business. That's why many times the deals end up being asset deals.

Asset Deals

I'll discuss the asset deal in more detail later, but let me touch on what it means. In an asset deal, you are buying customer lists, goodwill, fixed assets and all the equipment. In some cases, you're buying the accounts receivable or a portion of the accounts receivable that are on the books. You're buying the other company's inventory. You're buying all the other company's computers, the technology. You're buying maybe the trade name. Maybe you're buying a noncompete agreement, which might keep the other company's owner from getting back into the business for two, three, five years.

Those things are all important as you structure the deal. Which things do you have to have? What does the buyer want to keep? Maybe the buyer wants to keep some of the equipment. Maybe some of that stuff the buyer wants to keep for another purpose, or maybe the buyer has an unrelated side business for which he or she wants to keep some of the computer equipment or the phone systems.

Cash-Flow Financing

One way to do a deal is through cash-flow financing. If you recall, businesses this size sell for a multiple of cash flow. Cash flow, as we talked about earlier, is not necessarily net income. Net income is what larger businesses sell for. Cash flow is what the owner actually gets to take home, both in the way of actual cash, plus owners' discretionary expenses, plus any noncash items such as depreciation, interest, amortization—those sorts of things.

In cash-flow financing, you're potentially paying over a period of time. It could be a term note with owner financing. Perhaps you're paying 5 percent or 10 percent down and the remainder over 5, 7, 10 years. It's unlikely that you'll get 10 years. I'm not saying it doesn't happen, but it's unlikely. Typically, when the seller is ready to get out, he or she wants the money sooner for obvious reasons.

Sellers don't want to be in the loan industry. They would much prefer to have an all-cash deal. It's rare that you see a buyer who offers a seller a deal and the seller says, "No, give me it over 10 years," or, "No, I don't really need my cash now." It's the main source of income. It's the seller's largest asset. When they're getting out, sellers would much prefer to have an all-cash deal, or to have the buyers take on bank debt.

Cash-flow financing might be one of the seller's least favorite options, but it's one that has become much more popular since the recession. It's one that allows the sellers to get their money out over a period of time, plus they get interest, frequently at a decent rate. Even with bank interest rates at between 4 percent and 5 percent, you often will see the ex-owners receiving loan payments with interest rates between 6 percent and 9 percent these days. They're not going to get that interest anywhere else today in the United States.

In cash-flow financing, as you look at projections, the profit and the cash from the business you're buying has to be able to support the debt. You don't want to be using cash from your mother ship to pay for the acquisition. You'd love it if the purchase could be self-funded.

Now, it's a different matter if you're trying to take it to another level and you will be reinvesting to grow and expand the business that you are acquiring. But if you're simply adding this business on to your current one, it's important that it be self-sustaining. Otherwise, the model doesn't work, because you're going to be making less money the day after the deal, and that's not the idea. In this book, we're outlining a way to make more money the day after you make an acquisition.

Earn-Out

Another method is called an "earn-out." An earn-out, many times, is more of a contingent fee. What we talked about in cash-flow financing is almost like term debt. You've agreed upon the price, terms, and interest rate. It's just not a bank you're paying.

In an earn-out, the buyer may have doubts as to the price: "You have 30 percent of your business in one customer. What happens if that customer leaves me? Now I've bought a business that's reduced to 70 percent of the revenue and maybe 60 percent of the profit."

The earn-out might guarantee a certain dollar amount. Let's say the seller wants $1 million for his business. The buyer may say, "I'm only willing to guarantee $700,000 of that purchase price and I'll pay you that over five or seven years." The rest might be an earn-out, based on certain targets.

The earn-out concept is this: The buyer will pay the seller after the purchase, based on the company's performance and profitability. For instance, maybe I do better with the business than you did and instead of paying you the difference between $700,000 and $1 million—that $300,000 differential—I'm able to pay you $500,000 over the agreed period of time. An earn-out gives the seller the opportunity to gain some upside potential.

Usually an earn-out lasts between two and five years. It's typically based on the profitability or the growth on the top side revenue, after the buyer takes over. Often times, as I mentioned, it has a fixed component to it, which is 50–70 percent of the total purchase price. The rest is contingent on the buyer's performance, so the seller is taking some risk here.

The seller takes the risk that the buyer doesn't know what he's doing. Maybe the buyer fails. Maybe the buyer plays with the numbers and makes the business look unprofitable. All of those things are realistic concerns for the seller. That's why you have to make sure that you've done the dance and gone through the dating process we discussed earlier. You're into the final stages and you understand that the other party has a culture of trust and respect. You feel that the buyer is going to be straight with you.

Often in this earn-out option, the seller will stay for a time as an employee or in a specific role to help develop and grow the business. That could increase the potential that the earn-out could be bigger than the initial offer. The seller, typically, will stay for one to three years.

However, as the buyer, don't be surprised if the seller leaves much sooner. Sellers are used to running their own companies. They have been at the helm for years and often do not make the best employees. They're thinking, "Why are you doing that? I was successful for 30 years and didn't do it that way." Frustrated, they often quit.

You may want the seller to get out. I have often seen the buyer fire the seller long before the contract runs out. The buyer may not see enough effort on the part of the seller, who got a lot of money upfront and lacks the motivation for working for paychecks.

SBA Financing

A major financing opportunity for businesses in the $1 million to $30 million range is through the federal Small Business Administration, or the SBA.

The SBA is a government-backed program that guarantees 75 percent of the loan through a local bank. The SBA did that million-dollar deal for me in 2006. I only had to pay 10 percent out-of-pocket. The agency guaranteed 75 percent of the total funds, which means the bank didn't face much risk. It had my 10 percent and the SBA guarantee. The remaining 15 percent was owner financed.

That is great for businesses selling for under $2.5 million. It tends to be more constrained when businesses sell for over $2.5 million because of the loan guarantees, but for deals less than that the SBA often is the best option. The rates often are flexible, not fixed, but those rates are highly competitive.

Another advantage is that there is little annual reporting. Sometimes banks will require copies of tax returns, personal financial statements, maybe guarantees from individuals and financial statements from those individuals. They may also require audited financial statements yearly. With the SBA, the only requests I've ever seen are for copies of tax returns yearly, and to be frank, the SBA doesn't look at them. They're just a check-the-box organization.

A huge advantage is the low down payment. With a 75 percent guarantee from the government, the banks don't require as much down. Some of that down payment can come in the form of a seller note. For instance, in our 2006 deal, the bank had 75 percent guaranteed from the government, we put down 10 percent, and the seller held the other 15 percent, meaning we paid the seller just under $150,000 over seven years.

It's easy to qualify for these. You have to have good credit, though not necessarily great credit, but you don't have to have substantial assets and pledge substantial collateral to get these deals done. They will require personal guarantees, but afterward you're going to have a fairly risk-free loan with good terms that won't require a lot of yearly compliance. Typically an SBA loan is for 7 to 15 years, depending on whether it involves commercial real estate.

There are some disadvantages with an SBA-backed loan. One is that most times, the rates vary. As I write this in 2013, rates are low. However, few readers of this book think rates will be lower in 7 to 15 years. There is some risk in interest rates rising in that time.

Another disadvantage is the paperwork. It's not difficult, but it can be time-consuming. You will be asked for copies of licenses and birth certificates, and so on, to prove you're a citizen and that you qualify and that you are who you are. I remember closing a loan once in which I had to sign notes confirming that I was who I'd said I was on the previous page. Government at its finest.

Traditional Bank Financing

Traditional bank financing is another option, usually for shorter term debt. Five to seven years is more typical in a deal like that. These loans are typically available for decent-sized companies with better track records.

If you're the buyer, you might have stellar credit with good cash flow, and you're buying another business a bit smaller than yours, or maybe half the size, which will add cash flow. Maybe it's an asset-heavy business, with machinery and equipment. It might have inventory and substantial amounts of accounts receivable. Maybe it's got a big commercial building tied to it that you're buying. Any of those considerations make the deal more attractive for a regular bank.

It's true that regular banks do SBA deals also, but they do them with the government backing them. With traditional bank financing, you get out of doing that paperwork. One of the other disadvantages to an SBA loan is the closing time. Many times in an SBA deal, the closing isn't for 60 to 120 days. If you can get traditional bank financing, you might be able to close in 30 to 45 days, but you will need harder collateral assets and a good track record both for your business and the business you're buying.

Buying vs. Renting the Real Estate

Often deals in the $1 million to $30 million range will involve the purchase of real estate. Business owners don't want to pay rent for 15 or 20 years or however long they expect to run the company. They'd much rather buy, especially with attractive pricing and rates in today's market. We're seeing more and more businesses in owner-occupied space.

When they sell, they might not want to be a landlord and want the full liquidation. Maybe you don't feel like coming up with that capital today to buy it. In designing a deal, you need to decide whether you want to buy or rent the real estate. If you do want to rent it, the seller is likely to want a long-term lease to discourage you from moving. Sellers don't want to have to re-rent the space, so they might want a 5-, 7- or 10-year guarantee.

Banks often like real estate to be included. It's a hard collateral asset that they can liquidate in a sale, and so buying the real estate could increase the likelihood of easier financing. However, if it's a $2 million building, you might not have enough capital for the down payment. You will need to find the right balance to decide which way to go.

Should you, as part of the negotiation, work through a lease to buy? Do you say, "Hey, I'll take a three-year lease with a three-year option but at the end of year three, I've got an option to buy it as well, maybe at today's price"? That, too, will be part of your negotiations as you decide whether you want to be a property owner or a tenant.

Negotiating the Price

Negotiations always involve a give and take. It's similar to parenting. You can't get your kids to do everything you want. You've got to think about the most important things you want them to do and the values you want to instill, and press hard on those.

In the negotiation of an acquisition or a merger, each of you probably wants 10 things. You may only be able to get six or seven of those. If you only can get four of them, it's probably a deal you shouldn't do. It doesn't mean you definitely shouldn't do it. Maybe those four that you wanted are the best four and you can live without the other six.

Just be aware that you can't agree on everything and you can't get everything you want. If you can get everything you want in a deal, it's definitely a win-lose situation, and the other party, if correctly counseled, is not going to come to the table.

For example, if a seller wants $10 million and the buyer is adamant that the company is only worth $7 million, is the deal over? That could be short-sighted. You've made it to this point. You've gone through the due diligence. You've concluded that the cultures seem to be a good fit. You've already gone through these stages. It's late in the game to just give up. You need to pull on your boots and go to the table with a better idea.

If you're focused only on the raw numbers, you could miss out on a great opportunity. You can work with the numbers. You have to be able to negotiate. Each side has to be able to put itself in the other side's shoes. You have to say, "Okay, maybe it's not worth $10 million. Maybe it's not worth $7 million. What can we do to bridge that gap?"

Perhaps that $3 million difference could be contingent. As we discussed with an earn-out, that $3 million could depend on meeting performance goals after the buyer takes over. Or the payment could be delayed. Maybe it's cash-flow financing. Maybe it's a guaranteed deal but you get $500,000 now on that $3 million and another $1 million in three years and another $1.5 million five years later. Or perhaps the buyer would agree to the $10 million if allowed to pay the additional $3 million over a 7- or 10-year period. That could make all the difference.

The price, the timing, the payment terms—all those play varying roles in sealing the deal. They can be resolved through negotiation. What are things worth? For example, does the buyer want the seller to stay two years to transition? You can't ask the seller to work for free for two years, so you need to put a value on that.

We had a deal fall apart for a client who, as the buyer, kept asking and asking for things. The deal fell apart at the closing table because the buyer requested that instead of a two-month transition, which is what he had originally sought for free from the seller, he wanted a nine-month transition. That's basically asking someone to give up three quarters of a year for free. That was just too much. The seller said, "Forget it." She got deal fatigue. The buyer had just asked for too much. You have to be able to put yourself in the other person's shoes. Would you work for free for nine months? You need to be reasonable, or you can reach the tipping point where you upset the deal.

Like a Game of Chess

In designing the deal, think of it as fun. It can be like a strategic game, such as chess, with a lot of give and take. You can't get everything on your top-ten list, but you can get much of it.

You have to understand what your deal breakers are and how important the deal is for you and the other side.

Seeing the situation from the other party's perspective can give you an advantage in a negotiation. Recently, we went through a deal in which the buyer didn't need to buy, but the seller needed to sell. The business had not been listed for sale. The seller actually approached the buyer and sought a quick deal. The seller needed to close within 60 days for a few reasons, not the least of which was that the lease was running out.

The buyer, who didn't need the deal, made a low offer, thinking of it as a good little add-on that would increase the size of his company by about 3 percent. The seller came back with a purchase price that was more than 50 percent higher. The buyer returned quickly: "Listen, we understand the timing's important so we don't want to waste your time. If that's the price, we're not interested. I think it's time for you to talk to somebody else." It was not more than 10 minutes later when the buyer received a return phone call: "We'll take the deal you originally offered."

You have to recognize what is most important to you and which position you're in. Are you in a position of power, in which you don't need the deal, or do you have to sell? If you have to sell, you need to be careful about reaching too far. In the case I just described, the buyer probably would have accepted a counteroffer had it been only 10 percent or even 30 percent more. But the seller asked for too much. The buyer balked but ended up winning on the deal.

The average privately owned business changes hands every seven years. Remember that your business is your most important asset. My clients' businesses typically represent 65–90 percent of my clients' total net worth. A transaction like this can be the deal of your lifetime.

If you are the seller, it likely will be the largest transaction of your life. If you are the buyer, you need to understand that the seller feels strongly about a life's work and isn't likely to back down easily. Both the buyer and the seller need expert advice at this point.

CHAPTER 4

WHAT'S IT WORTH TO YOU?

O ne of my client's companies grew significantly over five years, from $2 million to $15 million. During that time, the company, a heavy equipment user, had to spend $6 million for equipment. As the company continued to expand, expand, expand, and invest back in the business, that growth has not necessarily been profitable.

The company didn't see a positive cash flow in that period causing the overall value to decline.

If that company were to liquidate today, the owner would have to come to closing with some cash to be able to afford to pay down the remaining debt on the equipment. It's a good example of the fact that just because a company is rapidly growing doesn't mean it is worth more. A company can indeed grow as much as that one did without adding value to its overall equity and value for an exit strategy.

The owner, realizing that the company, when we valued it, had gone backward significantly over the previous five years, put in place a strategy to change that around over the next few years and add investors and accelerate growth.

That's one example of how you cannot easily value a business when determining what it could sell for and what the market would bear. In this chapter, we will take a look at methods of business valuation, such as the cash-flow method, by which true entrepreneurial businesses in the $1 million to $30 million range are typically valued.

Fair Market Value

Fair market value of a company is often defined as the price at which property will change hands between a willing buyer and seller, both adequately informed of all the facts. Those terms often are negotiable in an actual transaction.

A company can be valued based on pure valuation. We do a lot of valuation work for gifts, estates, divorce cases, and business and legal issues that have nothing to do with buying or selling a company. However, when you're buying and selling a company, it's more negotiable. Sometimes a broker is involved. Sometimes the listing price is the starting point. The process takes into account a lot of variables and requires a number of assumptions.

In general, you will hear terms such as multiples of two to five times cash flow. How do we define that—and for specific industries?

We can't cover every detail of the topic of fair value in a chapter. Entire books have been written about it. However we're going to cover it in enough depth that you can understand where your situation might fit in and you can get an idea of what is reasonable as you work out the exact financial figures.

Cash Flow Multiples and Other Factors

Larger companies tend to trade for multiples of five to eight times cash flow. A strategy of buying three or four businesses could grow a company with half a million dollars in cash flow into a cash flow of $3 million to $5 million. They could be complementary businesses, they could be add-ons, or they could be up or down the distribution chain. Just by adding them together, you can get a much larger cash flow number. That will increase your returns significantly because the multiple you get upon exit will be significantly higher, perhaps reaching five to eight times cash flow.

Numerous other factors relate to the value of a company. It doesn't necessarily have to do with just top-line revenue. The larger companies, besides getting higher multiples, mostly are valued on earnings, not cash flow, because they have more stability, more back office, more systems, more processes.

You typically will look at the previous three to five years of data. However, sometimes something strange might have happened in the preceding year that's easily explained. For instance, maybe a company invested a ton in three new salespeople to the expenses, but they haven't gotten up to speed yet. Such things can be taken into account. Typically we look at three to five years of data for the target and see what that cash flow looks like.

It's not necessarily net income. What else is there? For instance, you can eliminate some expenses. We already discussed some owner discretionary expenses, such as excess travel, meals and entertainment and country club dues. There are other things that could be duplicative. For instance, if you're the buyer and you already have an office, do you really need to pay two rent bills every month? Maybe not. Maybe your space can absorb the new company. Maybe you don't need two office managers or two executive assistants or two salespeople or two marketing people.

It doesn't mean you're going to eliminate the expense right away. It might mean that you're going to test them both out for six to 12 months and see which is better. Over a period of time, whether that's six months or two years, you're going to be able to eliminate some of that duplication, thus adding cash flow.

Other factors that enter into the valuation include the nature of the industry. Some industries have been able to sell at extreme multiples. For instance, software as a service today is hot. As a monthly subscription model, it has been turned into a recurring revenue stream. These businesses are selling for multiples of top-line revenue instead of cash flow multiples.

Client concentration is another factor that weighs in. A significant piece of the business might be with one client—say, 20 or 40 percent. What happens to the buyer if that client goes away and 20 to 40 percent of the business disappears overnight?

With that level of client concentration, you might get a lower multiple, meaning you sell for less, or as the buyer you buy it for less. Or it could mean that piece of the business is contingent, and perhaps you don't guarantee that sale upfront. That is similar to an earn-out, which we discussed.

I had a client who bought a business in 2009 with 25 percent of the revenue from one large distribution company. The distribution company is highly profitable. There's no issue there. It's a $500 million company. However, shortly after, the distribution company had a changeover in management and philosophy and started to diversify. Instead of buying from one vendor, it started to buy from multiple vendors. The $3 million company that my client bought could have turned into a $2.2 million company almost overnight. Eventually, the revenue from that particular client was only 20 percent of what it had been. He hired an extra salesperson and never saw a drop in overall sales. Fortunately, the margin on that one customer was not high, so it ended up not affecting his bottom line nearly as much as it affected his top line. However, if he'd known that the client concentration was that high or that there was unrest in the management team, he probably would have made more of the deal contingent.

Other considerations include customer diversity, not just the concern of concentration, but whether sales are business to businesses or business to personal. Are you selling over the Internet? Do you have 100 customers, 10 customers, 1,000 customers? All that helps to define the business. The more customer diversity, the less likely you're going to lose all of your eggs quickly.

For instance, if your customer is a national retail store, it might have more control over its distribution channels and could object to your making a 20 percent margin, only agreeing to 15 percent. It may be able to squeeze you down more. It's hard for business owners to avoid that, considering the high volume such companies do. Nabbing 700 smaller customers might be more advantageous.

The time frame is another consideration. For instance, cash flow multiples and earnings multiples rose sharply in the mid-2000s and then dropped in 2008 and 2009 because of the recession. People were not buying companies. They were sitting on cash. Banks weren't lending, or so we were told. In 2010 we started to see those multiples rise. A lot of money had been on the sidelines from banks and private investors, hedge funds, and private equity groups. They only make money when their money is invested, and now they're coming back in droves to buy companies that are highly valued. They're buying them in larger multiples because they're back to competing to invest some of those dollars in solid companies.

Recurring revenue also factors into the value of a company. This doesn't necessarily mean cash flow. It could mean a different type of revenue stream in which you can count on repeating sales. The software-as-a-service industry subscription model, as I mentioned, is an example of that. Businesses that are revenue recurring, or that are seen that way, often are sold based on a multiple, whether that's 0.85 times revenue or five times revenue. Some of those software-as-a-service businesses have recently sold for 8 to 12 times revenue. A business that is doing $5 million in revenue might sell for $30 to $60 million over a period of time if it finds a strategic buyer interested in that market.

Another business that's like this is the CPA business, our business. CPA businesses sell based on a recurring revenue stream, every single time. I've never seen a transaction in the CPA model that doesn't base itself on recurring revenue. Because many people dislike changing CPAs, it ends up being, essentially, recurring revenue.

Another one is the financial services industry: people with assets under management, people who manage clients' money, people who do insurance work, life insurance, disability insurance, health insurance. Those are often considered recurring revenue businesses. Companies that get life insurance fees or something similar may sell for a smaller multiple, but higher multiples tend to be given for companies with a recurring revenue stream of assets under management in which a fee is collected each year based on those assets.

For a valuation, we also consider the general condition of the company. We look at the age and condition of the facilities. You want to be prepared for equipment changes, or for a leaking roof, as was the predicament of the client I mentioned earlier. As the buyer, you will want to know whether you face putting a couple hundred thousand dollars into your facilities because they're old or antiquated or because they don't fit the business model anymore.

How complete and accurate are the records? If a seller can't easily put his hands on the records, what does that say about his company? Does he seem to have it all buttoned down? Considering that he knew he'd be going through due diligence and questions would be asked, you would think the records would be in reasonable shape. If they aren't, maybe he isn't familiar with his own business or lacks the right personnel. Or maybe he's just short on time. But all those things can affect the value of the company.

What about employee morale and tenure? If key employees are not happy and are thinking about making a change, all they need is a new owner and they could have that extra motivation to change careers.

As for the tenure of employees, there are two sides to this. On the one hand, if they are all new employees, that could be a positive. If you're going to change the business, those employees might not be so set in their ways. It could also be a negative because maybe they don't know enough about the business model to be able to continue without the old owner.

But what if the tenure of those employees is 30 or 40 years? Do you have an employee base that's going to retire in the next three to five years? Perhaps you will have to think about replacing many of the staff, not just the owner. We recently consulted with a company in the financial services industry in which every employee was over 54. Now that may not seem old but when you have an entire staff base that's like that and they're all looking to transition over a 5- to 10-year period, you're talking about replacing an entire staff. Now you have nobody at the company who has a lot of experience with the clients.

If the employees haven't been there a long time, why not? What happened to the last person? Is this a continuing trend? Could this show you that maybe the owner isn't running the business with consideration for his people? Is the company running its people ragged? Is it treating them as if they were objects instead of helping them find the right work-life balance and career potential?

In our discussion of due diligence, I mentioned that reviewing resumes is a good idea, although not a must. You can get a feel for whether a person is a fit or not, or whether he or she should be moved to a new position.

It's tough, always, to measure these factors. Some are intangible, and sometimes the seller will not let you meet employees until after the deal has been consummated. We had an issue years ago in which the seller would not let us meet the staff until the day after the deal was done. When we introduced ourselves, two of the staff members broke down. They had thought that for sure the company was going to be transitioned to them in the next 5 to 10 years. They were blind-sided by the sale. We were able to get them on our side, but it took a while. It took trust. It took honesty. It took some hard feedback to be able to share with them why the sale happened.

Other factors in the valuation of a company can be the market demand and economic conditions. Economic conditions in most of the world have not been great recently, and they still affect companies in 2013. The bad times are reflected in the valuations, which look back on three to five years of performance.

The economic conditions of the industry can be important. Imagine if you had a printing company and were trying to sell it six or seven years ago compared with today. So many people print digitally. All of those industries are changing rapidly. If you have held on to your printer business for these last six or seven years, you've seen the industry change. Have you changed with the times? Have you changed with the industry? Business value in the printing industry has probably been significantly lowered over the last several years.

Are there intangibles in your business, things you can't neces-sarily put your hands on such as goodwill, or patents? Maybe it's the employee workforce. Maybe it's the culture. Maybe it's a significant client base. All these things can be intangibles. How do we readily transfer those to the new owner? If it's a patent and it's been approved and it's licensed, it's probably not as difficult to transfer, even if it was internally created. But if the patent was internally created, it's probably not on the balance sheet for a true value. It's probably on there for whatever legal fees and startup costs were incurred but not for the true intellectual capital put into that patent.

And how do you value the goodwill of the company? That is another thing that you can't necessarily see or touch on the balance sheet, but it's usually built into the cash flow of the company. Otherwise, clients wouldn't continue to return and buy products or services from these businesses.

Strategic buyers also will look at growth potential and future profits. If you're selling a company for $2 million, a strategic buyer who is running a $30 or $50 million company may want to get into your industry or your niche or your specific market area. Maybe that buyer is not in the metropolitan Chicago area but looking to get into that area. A truly strategic buyer may pay more than an individual investor. This may be a private equity group, it may be a hedge fund or it may just be a privately or publicly held company that is trying to expand its footprint or client base. Instead of buying for three to five times cash flow, they may buy for five to eight. Those deals are hard to find. There are few buyers in that market, and they only want the best of those businesses.

Buyers also are looking at the upside to the business. How much they pay will be based partly on what they think they can do with it, although those thoughts might not be shared with the seller. Maybe the buyer sees something stale or that the seller hasn't capitalized upon. The search engine optimization or products online or web presence might not be that great and the buyer plans to overhaul it.

As the buyer in circumstances like that, you might be able to say, "I know that they're making $200,000 or $500,000 a year and I know we're going to be able to increase that over time." Maybe that will require an investment in some new technology or in a new website, for example, but over time the buyer feels he can get that return on investment. He may have done it before.

Finally, are there any barriers to entry? For instance, is there product licensing? If you're a manufacturer and you have to go to China to manufacture, that's a pretty big barrier to entry. You're probably not going to see competitors jump up every day against you. However, if you're in the financial services industry, whether that's a CPA, an attorney, or insurance or financial advisors, those barriers aren't nearly as high from a cost standpoint. Maybe it takes a while to get a significant client base to make the living you want, but to truly enter the market just from scratch is not a significant cost.

Those businesses are going to sell for less, on average, than businesses with significant barriers to entry. The reason is that you might not be able to get into the latter. They may be government regulated, for instance.

Circumstances that Swing the Price

Other factors come into play when you're agreeing on a price. They might not be valuation matters, but they can have a significant role. One might be the specific circumstance of the buyer or the seller. I've mentioned a few such scenarios: The seller could be sick or dying or have some other compelling reason to exit the business, or a strategic buyer might pay extra to get into a niche and likes the seller's track record.

In such cases, if you're the seller, you don't want to tip your hand. If you're the buyer, you want to take advantage of whatever you can. The way to make money in anything is to buy low and sell high. In this case, you may be buying a business low and you may be able to sell it high when the market environment improves or you've tacked it onto your current business or you've cleaned up some things.

Another factor that could come into the price is the tradeoff between cash and terms. If the seller is willing to give the buyer more time to pay—say, 10 years instead of 5—that might be worth something to the buyer. It might be worth an extra $10,000, or $20,000 or half a million dollars, depending on the size of the deal. That helps the buyer's cash flow and requires fewer out-of-pocket expenses. Also, bank financing could be avoided.

Another consideration, which we will explore in the next chapter, is the tax consequences for the buyer and seller. Sometimes there could be a significant tax advantage or disadvantage to the buyer or seller and that could have an impact on the business changing hands.

One of our clients sold a company in 2012 for a few million dollars, most of which was taxable. After six months on the sidelines, this client was bored and wanted to buy another company, something different. The client acquired a company and made sure to do it before the end of the year, focusing less on negotiating terms with the seller and more on getting the deal done with end-of-year tax advantages for new equipment, costs and legal expenses. The advantage to the seller was not having to haggle over the final details on price or terms.

Three Approaches to Valuation

There are three main approaches to pure valuation: asset based, income based and market based.

Asset-Based Approach

The asset-based approach is rarely used when you're selling a company. It may be used in a heavy manufacturing business with high inventory and high accounts receivable, or in the real estate world where you have a significant real estate presence. Those are typically the criteria used in an asset-based approach.

The asset-based approach looks at the value of assets if you sold them off, maybe not the liquidation value but the fair market value of each tangible asset. You would be working with an asset appraiser, such as a real estate appraiser or an inventory or equipment appraiser, or some such specialist. It can be tough to value goodwill, the existing workforce and cash flow. It may be easy to identify those specific assets that show on the balance sheet—the equipment and inventory, the real estate—but it's hard to value those assets that aren't on the balance sheet at all.

I had a business that almost changed hands about a year ago. It was a significant business, with a balance sheet of about $60 to $70 million, most of it tied up in inventory and receivables. The business ended up not changing hands because the parties couldn't agree on the value. One wanted the balance sheet to take an asset-based approach and the other wanted it to be more of a cash flow model. The cash flow on the business was not quite as strong because the company had gone through some lean times over the previous couple of years.

The other two approaches, which we'll talk about a little bit more in depth, are much more common in the merger and acquisition space in the $1 million to $30 million company range.

Income-Based Approach

The income-based approach looks at the previous three to five years of data. The starting point is your net income. However, there are add-backs and subtractions for things that might go with the seller when the seller leaves, or things that the buyer may have to reinvest in. As we discussed, maybe there are things that the seller has let slide. Maybe technology hasn't been updated, or the office hasn't been updated in the last few years. Maybe it looks antiquated.

The income-based approach reflects anticipated future income benefits to the owner. It is based on historical analysis. Past performance is not a guarantee of future benefit, but it is the best model we have. There may be things the buyer can do to tweak or change or get some more cash flow out of the business, but none of that is taken into account for the purpose of pure valuation. The sellers, in many cases, won't even know what those things are. They generally don't care what the buyer is going to do with the business as long as they get their money and they keep their clients and employees happy.

There are lots of assumptions we make around the discount and capitalization rate of a company. They have to do with industry-specific issues, the customer concentration issues we talked about, and customer diversity. They have to do with growth potential. Is it a high-growth-potential business or is it a low-growth-potential business? What is perpetual growth? Over a long period of time, it's virtually impossible for a business to grow faster than the population grows in that area.

Market-Based Approach

The third approach is the **market-based approach.** This looks at data in the marketplace. You can buy subscriptions for data that is updated regularly on businesses that were sold or offered for sale over the preceding 5, 10, or 15 years, for any business in any U.S. industry.

You can differentiate by size, by cash flow, by revenue, by transaction value. All those things allow you to understand what's been out there, what's happened over time in this industry. That's what you're looking at in the market based approach. You're looking at what transactions have occurred, and what factors are similar to what you have as a seller. Then you try to decide how to value the company.

The tough part about this model is that it's hard to compare similar businesses because you don't know the circumstances. The data that is shared is pretty raw. You see the numbers, but you don't know if the sale was "distressed" because the buyer had to get out immediately. You don't know if the buyer was worried about capital gains rates increasing and so liquidated before the end of the year. You don't know if the business was purchased by a strategic buyer who paid more than the business was expected to sell for.

You would think that transaction data for companies similar in size, market and graphics would supply all this data, but it's slimmed down. Sometimes you have to make assumptions and you have to hope the businesses are similar when you're doing a valuation on a market basis only.

You also don't know how the noneconomic performance compares. Maybe the businesses had good staff; maybe it didn't. Maybe it had some patents you don't know about. Maybe it had some goodwill. Many times what's shared is revenue, overall transaction value, cash flow, net income and the region the business is in, but usually that's about it.

What happens if you run into a case where there have only been a few transactions, and they were several years earlier, perhaps during some of the worst economic years in decades. Are those even relevant? Maybe not. Getting that data can be hard.

Combining Approaches

What we often see in mergers and acquisitions is a combination of the income- and market-based approaches. A lot of times you'll look at both of them, come up with values separately, and then compare them.

You might observe something like this: "Well one's way out of whack; one's not. Why is that? Well, the data we had for the market-based approach is from 2008 and 2009. Or we must have missed some add-backs in our income-based approach." If the company lacks adequate cash flow, you may wonder if something is missing or the company hasn't invested in technology or done what other companies have done to stay competitive.

Whichever the approach or combination, it's important to understand how you're going to value the company in question and how those numbers relate to the cash flow you're going to get from the company. At the end of the day, you have to make sure that the deal makes sense for you. Again, it's not just a question of profit. The cash flow has to work in whatever financing you arrange. Get a good feel for the overall model and valuation method. Those approaches to valuation should come up with figures that are in alignment, and if they are not, then it's time for some further investigation.

Very few businesses actually change hands at true fair-market value. True fair-market value is conceptual. It's defined as the price at which property will change hands between a willing buyer and seller both adequately informed of all the facts. What if you're not adequately informed of all the facts? Does the seller know something he isn't revealing? Does the buyer have an unrevealed strategic plan for something he'll do as soon as the ink is dry?

It's rare that these businesses actually change hands at fair market value. Many times it's a strategic buy: it's based on the terms; it's based on the financing; it's based on some customer concentration; or it's based on getting into a new niche. All of those things factor in. It's not as easy as taking an actual multiple and saying, "My business is worth three times my cash flow." It's much more complicated.

This is where you need to get some professional advice and professional help. You need to get deep into the details. Understand what the market will bear and then try and find the right buyer—or seller—for the transaction. You want to be as knowledgeable as possible and come as close as possible to true market value by being well informed and by dealing with the right people and with the experts.

You need to make sure that somebody's on your side, whether you're the buyer or seller, because if the negotiations aren't handled right, I promise you the other party's going to get the better end of the deal.

CHAPTER 5

DANCING WITH UNCLE SAM

For those of you who just skipped to this chapter, thinking it might be the only one worth reading in a book on mergers and acquisitions written by a CPA, I suggest you go back and read the first four. However, if you're only going to read this chapter, I'll try to make it as interesting as possible.

Tax issues are extremely important in an M&A transaction. You can move significant dollars one way or the other. It's almost impossible to completely avoid Uncle Sam or the state taxing authorities. However, in a good transaction, advised correctly, you can save a lot of money.

We advised some financial services companies years ago, as they were doing a rollup strategy. They were buying business after business. Most of the transactions were based on goodwill but did include some equipment.

The equipment helped accelerate company growth by significantly lowering the tax burden in the early years. For instance, goodwill typically is a 15-year amortization item. As the buyer, you can only write off one-fifteenth each year after an acquisition. Equipment, however, can be written off over three, five, seven years, depending on what you buy. The tax code allows you to write off those initial investments, providing accelerated growth opportunities. You can instantly increase your cash flow over those early years by allocating more to the assets that you can depreciate faster and not giving that money to the government. This is all a timing difference, but keeping more cash in early years can help facilitate growth.

Earlier I wrote about the sale of a roofing company in which we moved nearly $400,000 to $600,000 off its tax bill. It all had to do with allocating between fixed assets, equipment, inventory and goodwill. In the case of this company, the company was the seller and we moved as much as we could to goodwill. The buyer was not getting competent advice.

A transaction like this is usually a zero sum game. From the IRS standpoint, it is extremely rare, if not impossible, that the buyer and seller can both win. Although we've talked about having to negotiate a deal and having win-win scenarios, when it comes to the IRS, typically you win or you lose or you've agreed upon something in the middle. Maybe, as the seller, you haven't got capital gains treatment on the whole thing, but you've made the goodwill allocation a significant portion. The goodwill can be a capital gains transaction for the seller.

These are some questions commonly asked upfront in a transaction: What am I going to get? Is this going to be worth it? Am I going to lose 40 percent of this to the government? That depends on the individual transaction, but working with good, competent attorneys,

CPAs, and brokers can help you eliminate as much of the tax load as possible and help you get your money up front.

The goal is to structure a deal in a way that's most advantageous for either the buyer or the seller. Because there are many kinds of transactions, this can be a negotiating point.

Stock vs. Asset Transactions

For businesses in the $1 million to $30 million value range, stock transactions are extremely rare, as I pointed out earlier. Stock transactions allow the seller to get capital gains on the entire transaction in almost every case. It allows the seller to easily transition the business to the buyer. The buyer takes over the entire company as is, by purchasing the stock. However, the buyer, in return, doesn't get to write off the price that he paid for the company until he later has a liquidation event. That might be many years later. If the average business changes hands every seven years, are you prepared to sit on your investment that long without any write off? It's not the best scenario for the buyer.

The few times we've seen stock transactions, they were due to unusual circumstances, for instance, significant contracts that couldn't be changed. Perhaps the buyer fears that a government contract underwritten by the seller will not be renewed if a new company is started. Those are the cases in which we see stock transactions most often. Even then, they probably account for only one out of 100 transactions in the $1 million to $30 million space.

The asset sale is much more common. Essentially, the buyer is purchasing every asset, including the ones that aren't on the balance sheet, such as goodwill, intangibles, patents, employee workforce and noncompete agreements. Of course, the inventory and equipment go with the deal, and sometimes receivables and payables as well. Sometimes the seller keeps receivables, collects the rest and pays whatever bills are due. It depends on the deal. It depends on the cash flow needs. A lot of that is negotiable.

This arrangement allows the buyer to then write off those assets at the purchase price. For instance, the buyer may purchase the company for $1 million, of which $200,000 may be equipment, $200,000 may be inventory, and the other $600,000 may be goodwill. That goodwill is written off over 15 years. Those 15 years can provide a significant write-off for the buyer. That $600,000 over 15 years is a $40,000 write-off each and every year for that business and that's not even a cash item, so the buyer can save significant tax dollars.

The equipment and the inventory can be written off much faster. The inventory, as soon as it's sold, will offset costs of goods sold and the equipment usually over 5 or 7 years. Those things, many times, drive the asset transaction.

Stock transactions are much more common with large businesses because it's just easier to transition. If you're doing $500 million in revenue, who wants to go to all those clients and all those vendors and start new contracts? It just becomes too complicated. But in the small business world of the $1 million to $30 million range, not that much paperwork or detail is involved, and you're not tied down in too many contracts.

Advantages for the Buyer

The buyer can save significantly on the front end in an advantageously structured deal. For instance, a financial advisory firm that was our client for a number of transactions paid very little income tax for those years when it was doing acquisitions.

It got significant write-offs on equipment. It also usually invested some dollars up front in updated technology or transition costs or a few extra employees for the period. It was rare that the firm had taxable income during that time.

The firm may have had a healthy cash flow, but the depreciation and amortization and interest on those acquisitions allowed it to significantly increase its write-offs, which weren't always cash related. Perhaps the firm paid cash for some smaller deals, so it wasn't out of pocket monthly, but it was able to get depreciation and amortization monthly. Or it might have had a deferred earn-out arrangement on some deals; it may not have owed anything in the first year but was still able to take ownership of those assets and write them off.

Typically, the buyer can shelter significant dollars and pay little in income taxes in the first two to five years of any deal. We recently had a client who had been an executive making half a million dollars a year and decided to buy a business. The client bought the business mid-year, and we were able to create a loss of almost a quarter million dollars. It was purely a tax loss. The client didn't actually lose cash, but we were able to accelerate deductions for some noncash items and take them in that first year. We were then able to carry back that loss to prior years when the executive was making significant money. We were able to get almost $100,000 worth of refunds from prior years. This provided the owner of this company with liquid assets for the next few years to reinvest in the business.

With the right tax strategy, you can lower income in the initial years of your acquisition, and that can create gains for you personally in cash and provide some liquid assets to build your business.

In those first few years, you often are investing in new people, new technologies, and new strategies. That costs money. How do you get that money? You get it by turning as little as possible over to Uncle Sam.

Specific Tax Strategies

Let's take a closer look at some of the tax strategies that can be used in the buyer-seller transaction. In particular, we'll look at installment sales, the transaction structure, and the balance of capital gains vs. ordinary income. Also, we'll consider strategies when real estate is involved in the deal. Will it be a sale, a lease, or somewhere in between?

Installment sales. They often involve either owner financing, or the earn-outs that we have discussed. They also can be used to create tax advantages that can help to seal the deal. This is the common way for a seller to get a portion of income immediately, but it may be normalized over a three-, five-, or seven-year period to avoid bumping into a higher tax bracket.

The seller then reports this income as it is received. Let's say it's a $1 million transaction, and for simplicity of illustration, the seller gets $100,000 a year with no interest over 10 years. That puts the seller in a lower tax bracket. It allows the seller to pay less over a period of time and maybe budget for and plan for those tax items without one big pop.

Many times, unless a transaction occurs in January, the seller has a major tax burden in the year the company sells. That is because most businesses in the small to medium-sized income range are cash-basis taxpayers, and they do everything they can to pay as little tax as possible each year.

If you no longer own a business at the end of the year, there is not much you can do to defer your income. There's no new equipment to buy, no new cars, no extra expenses at the end of the year. When you still owned the business, it may have had a sizable income. You face taxes on that, as well as on the proceeds from the business sale. It's like a double whammy in the year of the sale. By receiving your proceeds in installments, you can spread the income out for years. Be aware, however, that laws could change and the prevailing laws in the years you receive the funds are the tax rates you are stuck with, not the laws in the year you sold.

There are a few exceptions to the installment sale rules. I won't go into too much detail here because you should consult your tax advisor, but there are specific exceptions for inventory, accounts receivable, and depreciation. Those items become income immediately. These are often called hot assets. They are assets that would have otherwise created ordinary income to the seller. Because they would have created ordinary income, they can't be recognized in an installment sale. They would be taxable in the year they were sold whether the seller received the cash or not.

Another reason installment sales can be attractive for the seller is that the seller can earn interest. A 6 to 9 percent interest rate is fairly typical. As I write this book, most interest rates in the United States are under 1 percent, so if you can get a 6 percent to 9 percent rate on your money, it's a pretty good investment. Granted, there are risks, but that's true of any business transaction.

Transaction structure. Buyers want to buy assets, and sellers want to sell stock. We talked about this at the beginning of this chapter. Buyers want to buy assets because they can depreciate and amortize them faster. Sellers want to sell stock because they get to recognize it all as capital gains. However, 99 percent of closely held businesses are asset sales. It's just a reality.

Another issue is the seller's status as a C corporation, an S corporation, or an LLC. They each have distinct tax ramifications when it comes to a sale. The details are too extensive for a book on mergers and acquisitions strategy. However, suffice it to say that no matter which type of corporation you own, you should have thorough discussions with your professional advisor. C corporations, for instance, have no capital gains. It doesn't matter how much goodwill you sell, there are no capital gains at the C corporation level in an asset sale.

That's an example of why it's important to make sure you understand your current corporate structure. If you're 5, 7, 10 years away from a potential liquidation, you should have a discussion with your attorney, your CPA, or other professional counsel on what the strategy should be if you were to sell. It's always better to have that discussion now than it is to wait until you're in the process of selling, when nothing can be done to change your structure.

In an asset sale, the way those assets are allocated will play a huge role in your tax savings. How much of the value, for example, will be attributed to fixed assets, and how much to goodwill? Buyers want as much value as possible to be placed on the fixed assets, the equipment, the inventory, the receivables—the assets they can get a faster return on. Sellers, on the other hand, want as much value as possible to be placed on goodwill.

Everything is negotiable in a transaction once you've gotten to this point. Once you've explored the culture fit and done your due diligence, you have now moved on to designing the deal, its structure, financing and allocation. All those items are negotiable. The key here is you want to be at least as informed as the other party in the transaction. The less informed you are, the more you risk losing out on potential opportunities.

Capital gain vs. ordinary income. The tax on capital gains in the United States can range anywhere from zero percent up to 23.8 percent. A lot depends on your individual tax strategy and tax bracket.

Much has been written on how all that works. Just understand for tax savings, capital gains are, on the whole, significantly better than ordinary income, for which the tax can range up to 43 percent in the United States. That's just the federal side for both the capital and ordinary income. And that, of course, is why, as the seller, you want as much of the deal as possible in capital gains.

Again, it's a negotiation. What types of items are categorized as capital gains? Stock could be one such item, if you can persuade the buyer to accept stock in your company. In an asset deal, depending on how the contract is written, capital gains could include intangibles such as goodwill, patents, employee workforce, and noncompete agreements. A capital gain includes the price at which you sell equipment for more than what you originally paid.

For instance, depreciation recapture is a term that often confuses sellers. Let's say you bought equipment for $100,000 and you've depreciated $50,000. If the buyer pays you $100,000 for that equipment, you're going to have a taxable gain of $50,000. That's going to be ordinary income because that's the amount you depreciated. The IRS is basically saying: "You got an ordinary deduction of $50,000 over time because we thought the equipment would be worth less when you sold it. However, it's worth the same amount, so give us back the deduction that we gave you as ordinary income." Again, it's a zero sum game. The IRS, historically, hasn't allowed you to take an ordinary deduction for something for which you later pick up capital gains income when you sell it.

It's important to understand the corporate structure and where you have room for give and take. Buyers prefer ordinary income because they can write it off quicker than capital gains. For instance, intangibles, typically, are a 15-year amortizable asset whereas ordinary income items—inventory, accounts receivable, and some of the fixed asset costs—can be written off much faster.

When you're the seller of a business, the things that can stick you with ordinary income include the debt the buyer assumes. For instance, if you're transferring your line of credit to the buyer, or you're transferring your accounts payable or your bank debt, all of those things are considered additions to the purchase price. If you're receiving $500,000 in cash and you're giving up a $200,000 debt that you no longer have to pay off, then you're receiving $700,000 of value.

Inventory is an ordinary income item because it is treated as if you were selling it to an ultimate end customer. You should have some basis in that inventory and you might be able to take a loss. Maybe you have $500,000 of inventory on the books, but the buyer's not going to purchase it for $500,000. Maybe the buyer will purchase it for 80 percent of that amount. Call it $400,000. That's good for you, as the seller, because you're going to get a $100,000 loss on the sale of your inventory.

Accounts receivable can result in ordinary income if you are a cash basis taxpayer. They are treated no differently than if your customer paid you. Perhaps the buyer is paying you 75 cents on the dollar for what was owed and will take care of the collections. That's ordinary income to you. If the buyer is paying you 75 cents on the dollar, you may have an ordinary loss, if you are an accrual basis taxpayer.

Real Estate Sale or Lease

In a real estate transaction, is the real estate going to be sold with the business or is it going to be leased, or some combination of the two? Selling the real estate allows a seller to cash out and pick up income all at once and not have to deal with being a landlord. There are advantages to that.

On the tax side, the amount of the depreciation comes back as ordinary income to the seller. However, if the buyer purchased the building for $1 million and can now sell it for $1.5 million, that $500,000 appreciation is treated as capital gains.

The seller may choose to lease the property to the buyer, typically for 5 to 10 years. That allows the income to be smoothed out over a longer period. Earlier, I pointed out that sellers face a double whammy on taxes if their business had a large profit in the same year that they sold it. On top of that, selling the real estate could lead to a triple whammy. A lease would provide the seller a guaranteed stream of income, evened out over time. Meanwhile, the property still is a write-off if it carries a mortgage, condo fees, or other expenses.

The seller also would have future appreciation or depreciation, depending on which way the real estate market went. If you had sold your company in 2007 and kept the real estate, you may have seen a significant decline in the value of that real estate over the next few years. Hopefully, by the time you're reading this book, the value has come back.

A common option involving real estate is this: If the buyer doesn't have the funds to put down on both the business and the real estate, he may lease with an option to buy. The option might come at the end of a three-year lease or a five-year lease. Typically, the option to buy would be at today's market value because the buyer is guaranteeing the seller a rental income and a buyout after three to five years. Knowing that it will be at today's market value allows the buyer to project out for future income purposes, and allows her to plan for that tax event that she knows is going to happen in the next few years. It also gives the buyer time to understand the business model before plunking down additional cash on the real estate.

Whether it's a real estate sale, lease, or option to buy, the arrangement can be personalized within the deal. Once again, everything is negotiable. There can be advantages for the buyer to buy the building with the business. One advantage is financing. As I mentioned earlier, the financing often is easier if a commercial building is attached to the business sale.

That was the case for a buyer we worked with several years ago. It was SBA financing, and it was one combined loan for the building and business, with a repayment term of about 16 years. It had to do with the value of the business, the value of the real estate, the combined value, and what the SBA would do. It allowed the buyer to increase the loan term and cash flow in those early years instead of being stuck with a seven to ten year term on the acquisition. SBA financing can be an especially good opportunity for a business deal when real estate is involved.

Common Questions

Common tax questions always come up in a deal. How much will I get to keep? How can I save on taxes for the transaction? Do I have to pay it all at once? Can I income average for tax purposes? How much gifting can be employed to my advantage? Are banks' lending money now?

The answers to those central questions of how much you will get to keep and how you can save on taxes will depend on the transaction structure, on whether it's an installment sale, the amount of capital gains and the amount of ordinary income, and if you are the seller, whether you can force more of the value toward goodwill instead of the equipment.

"Do I have to pay it all at once?" Yes, if you are going to do a full cash transaction, but you could avoid that with an installment sale, an earn-out, or a note payable over a two- or three-year period.

"Can I income average?" This is one of the top questions I'm asked. Income averaging hasn't existed in 30 years, yet people remember it and wonder if it's still available for them. It's all pre-Reagan tax code. When people ask this question, it tells me that they knew something about taxes a long time ago and then got caught up with other concerns as the tax laws changed.

"How much gifting can be employed to my advantage?" If you're asking this question during the transaction, it's likely too late. However, this is why this book is so relevant for the buyer and the seller. You should be thinking about this in advance. You should be talking to your counsel.

If you're three, five, seven, ten years away from thinking about selling, you can gift some of the shares of your company as a strategy to your children, siblings or whomever you choose. Those gifts don't necessarily give you current deductions. You don't get a charitable deduction for gifts to relatives, but it's a way to shift wealth significantly from one generation to another. There's far more to that than I could hope to cover in this book, but understand that it is a potential strategy for shifting wealth, not necessarily tax dollars.

"Are banks' lending money now?" Since the end of 2011, we've seen a turnaround in the M&A space, and banks are lending on good deals every day. It's another reason you need to get your business in shape for a potential sale.

Keeping It Clean

I come back to the old saying, "You can't have your cake and eat it too." You can't cheat the IRS and then hope to sell your business for a multiple of that cheating. You will recall that dry cleaner I mentioned earlier in this book. He was trying to sell his business based on a multiple of cash flow but couldn't prove the cash flow because the tax returns didn't show it. The implication was that he was taking cash on the side.

You can't think about this transaction as a way to cheat the IRS. What we try to do is work every advantage possible to pay the IRS as little as possible as late as possible.

Good advice is essential. That might not be from your current CPA. You would do well to work with somebody who has a presence in M&A transactions. Not every CPA does them. We get referrals many times from local CPAs who don't deal in this world on a day-to-day basis as we do.

I suggest you get good advice because the dollars are significant. The sale of a business likely will be the largest transaction in the owner's life. This is the owner's baby, and it's most of the owner's net worth. Depending on the size of the transaction, making an error without competent advice can cost thousands, tens of thousands, hundreds of thousands of dollars.

For the buyer, saving those dollars is important. You need the right advice on allocation of sales price, structure, and time frame. All of those can make a major difference, especially in the earlier years after you've done the deal.

CHAPTER 6

LANDING A GOOD CATCH

We painted a picture of how we wanted to look, a vivid portrait of success and growth. And when we shared that picture with others, opportunities opened.

It was several years ago, as my firm continued to look for acquisitions, that I happened to hear a great speaker named Cameron Herold. He urged entrepreneurs to envision that "painted picture" of what their world would look like in three to five years. We took that to heart. In our picture, our firm would be almost doubling in size in that period, and we would have multiple locations. At that time, we had only one.

We spread the word, and within six weeks one of those with whom we shared our vision told us about another business that was less than happy and was looking for a change. We were introduced, and six months later we looked almost like our picture. The key was to share our ideas and ambitions and how we wanted to get there.

In this chapter I will focus on how to find a good deal. You don't usually come across one deal and immediately do it. Sometimes you need to look at 5 or 25 possibilities before you find one or two to pursue. How do you come across that many prospects?

There are a lot of good opportunities out there. Sometimes they're easy to find, sometimes they're harder to find, but as long as you are consistently thinking about them, you will find those opportunities over time. They don't always hit you right in the face like the ones we were lucky enough to come across a couple of years ago, but eventually they show up if you are continuously mining for them.

Many times, the best deals don't hit the market. They aren't on a website. The owner isn't advertising to sell. On many occasions we've found deals that weren't listed. The companies weren't for sale, but you could find a way to make a deal happen.

Brokers

So how do you do this? There are so many ways. When we were just getting started in 2004, we did it in obvious ways. We consulted websites and business brokers. And we didn't stop there. Over the next year, we formed relationships with some key brokers. Many brokers sell only in specific industries. For instance, four or five brokers specialize in selling CPA firms, and that's all they do. They don't usually list other businesses. That's the case for many industries.

So it's not just about mining the websites and looking at the websites, which back in those days I would do weekly. We've built those relationships. Those folks will let us know before they even have a deal signed. They'll say, "We think we're going to have something in your area. We think it's a fit for you."

And we've informed them of what we're looking for over time. "If you find something in a certain area that's doing certain types of work," we say, "we will almost exclusively buy it every time." They understand that we can get a deal done. Many times, merger and acquisition brokers work on a contingency fee. They get paid only if the deal gets done, so they're highly incentivized to find a good buyer who's going to be honest with them and give them a quick yes or no. They dislike the slow yes or the slow no—especially the slow no—that wastes their time with just a lot of talk.

Introducing yourself to local business brokers or specialized industry brokers is the number-one way to get started in the M&A space. We started that way, and that's the way we recommend a lot of our clients start. It gives them an easy introduction to the M&A world.

You can move from there, as I said, and share more information. And if you're looking for ways to find good brokers in your area and you're not sure, I can tell you it's fairly easy. Ask your CPA, ask other CPAs, or ask attorneys or bankers in the area. They know which ones are the good brokers, and by good brokers, I mean they regularly have good deals. They have good deal flow. They're reputable. They're trustworthy. Those are all important traits in a broker because you can waste your time with many brokers: as you look at the deals they find, you realize you're not looking at good data.

Advisors

Local bankers, attorneys, and CPAs often know when someone is thinking of selling and can make an introduction to a buyer. Inform them that you are looking to grow and ask if they know anyone in the industry looking to exit, maybe to retire or switch careers. They may often know because they have clients in your industry. Once they think about it, some good prospects can emerge.

In 2005 and heading into early 2006, this occurred for us. We had done a deal with a CPA who then became a broker, and we had said we would continue to acquire businesses. Six months later, his old business partner was looking to sell, so he approached him immediately: "I know the buyer for you."

We were able to get that deal done quickly without it ever hitting the market because we continued to talk to people who could make those introductions for us. Over time, bankers, attorneys and CPAs gain a lot of access to business owners in a variety of industries, and often they know of a deal brewing before it ever gets to the broker.

Industry Networking

A third way is to network with people in your specific industry. That can be done through local meetings. For instance, maybe you have an industry group that meets quarterly or monthly in your area or at national conferences. We do this fairly often for CPA firms. We go to industry meetings in the North Carolina and South Carolina region, and we also network at national meetings. We let small groups know that we're looking to continue to grow through mergers or acquisitions or by adding partners. You'd be surprised how many times people say something like, "I know someone who might be interested. My cousin's CPA is turning 65 next week and I don't think he has an exit strategy."

People want to help you. It is human nature to want to help others succeed, and it makes people feel good to be able to make an important introduction. Networking is a great way to get some industry data, quickly share, and maybe do a deal that never even hit the market.

As I pointed out earlier, 96 percent of businesses that have been sold are still operating five years later. That's an important message of this book because it is one of the key reasons why mergers and acquisitions can be a highly effective way to grow.

Direct Marketing Campaigns

Another way that you can grow is to do a direct marketing campaign. The cost is relatively cheap. You can do it with postcards or letters. We've done it with letters over the years. It may be a couple of paragraphs describing who you are, what you're doing, and how many times you've done an acquisition, and explaining that you're looking to grow and why.

You know some of your competitors in your area, and you know if they're struggling, not growing, burned out, or close to retirement. You're aware of these people as you do your marketing data. They're listed in your local business journal as the top 25 in that area, and they win awards, but as you follow them, you find yourself thinking, "I don't think they have an exit strategy."

We follow up regularly with letters. We send letters every six months to 30–50 competitors in the area. Perhaps the owners are of a certain age. Maybe we know their business hasn't been as successful for the previous couple of years as it used to be. We may know they've been hit by the economy. We've made inquiries through clients who have switched firms. Based on what we hear, we may reach out to other CPAs to see if they need some help, and whether we can make a connection.

After spending time on the initial writing, you can then reproduce those letters every six months for just the cost of a stamp. We've made three acquisitions just by sending those letters, and we've had countless other meetings at which we decided not to do the deals.

One recent January morning, after the holidays, I came into my office to a message on my machine. The caller said he had kept our letter for the last three years and figured we seemed aggressive enough to be a potential fit in the future. He had kept it next to his computer for three years, and when the time was right, he picked up the phone. In this particular case we did not end up doing the deal. It wasn't a great fit. But it's impressive that something like that can result from a postage stamp.

When you're thinking about this as an active strategy, you can enlist your marketing and salespeople to help you. We've enlisted our marketing and salespeople regularly because they go to networking events. They see other CPAs. They see other folks in the industry. They'll see people locally. They'll meet people at golf tournaments, for example, and we want them to share the message about what our firm aspires to do.

They've also been enlisted to help with the letter writing and the mailing. It gets them excited because they're not just focused on winning new clients but they're also helping us grow the business in a significant way through acquisitions.

Always Be a Buyer and a Seller

You should always be a buyer, and you should always be a seller too. Don't be so much in love with your business that you can't see a great exit opportunity.

I was reminded of that recently by an 83-year-old at MIT's Entrepreneurial Masters Program. He has built an incredible amount of businesses over the years. He's known as the franchise guru in the United States. He suggested that you always want to be both a buyer and a seller because if somebody comes along with a good deal, you don't want to be so attached that you miss out on it.

Consider this: What if you're having a discussion and you think you're going to be a buyer and somebody makes you an incredible offer to be a seller because you've done such a good job building your business?

It's important to always remember that unless you're one of the few who are building a lifestyle business or transitioning the business to the next generation, you're essentially building this business to exit it at some point. As your business gets bigger, you want to make sure that you're building the business in the right way so the multiples grow. You want to preside over a business that's built to sell.

The baby boomers who have built businesses are going to provide the largest opportunity ever for mergers and acquisitions over the next 10 years. As they exit the workforce, you're going to find buying opportunities. Make sure you engage your marketing and sales team and all of your people in the acquisition mode. We share regularly the deals that we're looking at and what's going on in our firm. And we share that with everybody so that they will be thinking about us when they hear of something. It's Cameron Herold's painted picture philosophy.

Life is in the approach. You're looking at deals and searching for good ones. Though this chapter is near the end of the book, it is of prime importance. If you don't ever find a deal, you will never have a need for chapter one. You have to land the catch before you can fry the fish.

It's all about relationships and building rapport. Whether you are the buyer or seller, you have to build your relationship. It's a question of letting the other party know that you can handle this deal, that you've done this before, or you have competent advisers to see you through it.

THE DONE DEAL

Throughout this book, I have driven home the lesson that you have to avoid the big mistakes. You may assume that I mean financial mistakes, but I mean much more than that. I believe that ensuring a good corporate culture fit is most important, and that's why I began the book with that emphasis.

You have to make sure you've done due diligence not just on the financials but on the corporate culture as well. You need to examine the range of HR issues as well as the cash flow. Are the people going to get along? Who will have which responsibilities? When you embark on a deal of your own, I suggest that you review all these chapters to make sure you aren't overlooking something major.

You then have to focus on the actual acquisition and how to finance it and design the deal and the tax strategies. The focus often ends up on the asking price, and you can take a hard stance, but that's not always the best approach. Everything is negotiable, whether it's the overall price, the terms, the interest rates, or the ultimate responsibilities of buyer or seller.

The way I often like to look at a deal is through cash flow, when we get to that point. The buyer shouldn't be greedy. A cash flow model can show whether the buyer is going to be able to cover the debt and add cash flow, potentially $30,000, $50,000, $70,000, $100,000 more, starting on day one. If that's the case, and if the seller wants X, Y or Z, maybe the buyer should consider giving on those points. After all, once he owns the company, he's going to be making more money.

Sometimes a business owner thinks his baby will sell overnight. But it can take time, and sometimes the business isn't ready to sell. You have to make sure you've built a company, not a job. A job earns you money, but you're not acting as a business owner so much as an employee. If you've built a true company with systems and processes, it'll be easier to sell.

Maybe the seller has failed to take personal goals into account when planning an exit. She thought she could retire and sell the business for a million dollars and that's what she needs, but that might not be what the business is worth.

Or the seller fails to consider how the buyer is thinking about the deal: as a job, an investment, or as a business opportunity. The seller ignores his own exit plan, or doesn't have one at all. Many times the seller has just gone day by day by day until he is burned out. A buyer can take advantage of that lack of planning and foresight. The seller should have built the business from day one with the exit in mind. You never know when something's going to happen to you personally, professionally, or somebody's going to come along with a great deal.

I recently heard a powerful speaker named Deb Roy, who was fortunate enough to have Twitter buy his company. Roy built his company over the last four years and had a good exit. His company wasn't even for sale, but he agreed to meet with Twitter anyway because he was open to hearing the story. Twitter acquired his company for a significant number. Roy had built the company to sell. That sale just came sooner than he had expected.

Good for Both Parties

After the deal is done, you have to be sure you're ready to proceed. How do both parties feel about the deal? Do you have a good working relationship? How important will that be? Is the seller going to stay on board for 6, 12, 18 months? If so, you don't want to burn bridges or take too many hard stances as the buyer because you will need to work together. Now all of a sudden you're going to turn on the charm and be nice right after the deal?

You don't want the seller to feel sold, as if you got one over on him. It's best if both buyer and seller feel they had some give and take. The deal has to be good for both parties. If it's a win-lose, usually that means someone needed the deal so badly that he couldn't go on without it.

Each party has to be clear about what's in the deal for her. For the seller, that's likely to be a profitable exit with employees pleased and reputation intact; for the buyer, it could be cash flow, extra support, new processes and system, or a new niche. Or the buyer may want the deal for the equity of a bigger company—in other words, it's time to take the company to the next level, and this is the path for growth.

The Personal Touch

For the seller, the deal represents a life's work. Sellers build their companies with their blood, sweat and tears, and this is an emotional time. The seller wants to be a good steward to the clients and employees, making sure the buyer will take care of them.

"It's just business, so don't take it personally," people often say, but for an entrepreneur in this $1 to $30 million range, business is quite personal. The people and the families know one another. They know the employees' kids. They know their clients' kids. They've been to dinner with these folks. They've been to weddings. And that's why it requires such a personal touch, not just on the buyer's side but also from your advisers, from your bankers, your CPAs, your attorneys. Whoever it is—an investment banker, a business broker, your marketing and sales team—must understand that this isn't a boxing match where one side gets knocked out and the other side jumps and cheers. The transfer of a company calls for finesse from all involved.

How We Can Help

As we conclude, I'd like to say a few words about our firm and how we might help you. As of this writing, we have looked at over 80 deals and closed ten. We also advise on 15 to 30 deals a year both on the buy side and the sell side.

We've helped clients all across the country. We specialize in the Southeast, but much of what we do can be accomplished via Skype, telephone and email. We certainly can meet face to face whenever necessary.

We work with both buyers and sellers. About 70 percent of the time our buyers have found a target and they're looking for advice on how to proceed. We can help with planning, strategy, culture, due diligence, designing the deal, and working out financing and tax issues. We help with SBA, owner financing, earn-outs, and we have helped to close deals with angel investors and private equity groups and hedge funds.

About 30 percent of the time, people are just getting started. They may feel stuck and want to accelerate their growth rate, and they see that we've done this a lot. For those clients, we're starting with the last chapter in the book, which is how to find the right deal and the right people to get it done.

We advise them of considerations up front such as how much cash flow they could add to their business, the down payment they may need, the tax advantages, and more. We can start wherever the buyer or seller is in the process.

Sellers sometimes tell me they have a lifestyle business that can't be sold, but it's often not the case. I've seen it often. People will pay to get $150,000, $250,000, $500,000 of cash flow. And despite sellers' concerns, their clients tend to stay with the buyer; it's much easier for them than finding a new company to trust.

We often advise sellers on how to prepare for the best deal. We talk about the systems they should have in place, the time frame for the sale, and how to attract buyers. We talk about whether or not to go through a broker or an investment banker.

We help with due diligence and cultural issues. For example, we're not technology experts, but we do know you need to make sure you're paying close attention to compatibility issues. We might not be HR experts, but we know that if two employee manuals seem like polar opposites, you need to be cautious about whether the cultures of the two companies could ever work together. You just don't get that advice many times from others, whether that's your CPA, your investment banker or your attorney.

We can help with the market conditions for an industry or for the general economy. Back in the troubled economy of 2008 and 2009, we actually found out it was one of the best times to go on the warpath for a merger or acquisition. We doubled and tripled our efforts and acquired three businesses in a short amount of time. We find that when other people are struggling or when other people are running, you should look for opportunity. That perspective has continued to serve me and my clients repeatedly in a positive way.

You're always looking to buy low and sell high, just as in the real estate market or the stock market. Down times often are good times for you to buy, not sell. In fact, the sellers out there may find that you are the only buyer in your market.

As for financing options, we've helped, as I mentioned, with earn-outs, SBA, owner debt, and we also look at who's lending in the market. Back in 2008 and 2009, even struggling banks were lending in certain deals. They were still lending, for instance, in SBA deals, especially in an acquisition that let them shore up their balance sheet with a 75 percent government guarantee. We've seen local banks in our area continue to expand their presence, especially in the SBA world. They've been looking to lend as much as possible since 2010. We can make introductions to banks in those areas. We have a network through CPA firms and attorneys across the country that are aligned with banks. That gives us a wide reach.

Finally, we can help with structuring the deal and making sure, as I have shared throughout the book, that we find the tax advantages. I'm not talking about saving $1,000. We can sometimes save hundreds of thousands of dollars in the way the deal is designed and the write-offs are timed.

Our job is to advise you on what is negotiable—and that is almost everything—but to stop short of taking a hard stance. You can take a hard stance on something that would break the deal for you, or when you know the other side has no choice, but those situations are few and far between.

Keep in mind your top-ten list of what you want to get out of the deal. But even as you concentrate on that list, remember that the other side has one too. If you can reach most of your goals, you likely are doing well and can proceed with confidence. Be a deal maker, not a deal breaker.

APPENDIX

The Due Diligence Checklist

- Nondisclosure agreement
- Three years of tax returns
- Three years of financials
- Revenue by month for a three-year period
- Salaries per person
- Staff duties
- Average raises
- Bonus structure
- Benefits
- Hourly billing rate by person
- HR policies
- Paid time off
- Owner perks

- Insurance
- Software
- Services performed
- Time reports for three years
- Receivables
- Collection policies
- Billing policies
- List of equipment and when purchased
- References
- Start-up cash needed
- Inventory
- Research
- Bank debt

How can you use this book?

MOTIVATE

EDUCATE

THANK

INSPIRE

PROMOTE

CONNECT

Why have a custom version of *Cracking the Code?*

- Build personal bonds with customers, prospects, employees, donors, and key constituencies
- Develop a long-lasting reminder of your event, milestone, or celebration
- Provide a keepsake that inspires change in behavior and change in lives
- Deliver the ultimate "thank you" gift that remains on coffee tables and bookshelves
- Generate the "wow" factor

Books are thoughtful gifts that provide a genuine sentiment that other promotional items cannot express. They promote employee discussions and interaction, reinforce an event's meaning or location, and they make a lasting impression. Use your book to say "Thank You" and show people that you care.

Cracking the Code is available in bulk quantities and in customized versions at special discounts for corporate, institutional, and educational purposes. To learn more please contact our Special Sales team at:

1.866.775.1696 • sales@advantageww.com • www.AdvantageSpecialSales.com

Printed in the USA
CPSIA information can be obtained
at www.ICGtesting.com
JSHW012037140824
68134JS00033B/3118